This book shows that good requirements and digital solution design are seamlessly connected. An essential read for all business analysts who wants to make an impact with well-designed digital solutions.

Rob Onink BSc, BCS Advanced Int. Diploma in BA and
Lead Business Analyst, Netherlands Enterprise Agency

Relevant, current and comprehensive 'how to guide', highlighting up-to-date research and a variety of in-depth defined models to inform the audience of best practices on designing digital solutions. I thoroughly enjoyed the relevant examples used throughout the chapters, which can be applied across many roles within the digital solutions world. Can't recommend it enough, regardless of what stage of your career you're at, this book is bound to be useful.

Florina Cretu MSc BSc, Business Analyst,
RSA Insurance, part of the Intact Group

Designing Digital Solutions is a clear, practical guide that bridges strategy and execution – essential reading for anyone driving digital change in today's complex environments.

Erivan de Sena Ramos, Business Analysis Leader in Tech,
CBAP, PMI and CSM Certified

Designing Digital Solutions establishes itself as a practical reference book for those designing holistic digital solutions. Framing all aspects of user interface, process flows, cybersecurity and more, into a comprehensive blueprint for delivering sustainable digital experiences. A must-have for students and professionals seeking structure and clarity in the solution design process.

Amal Taibouni, Director of Technology, Unifi LD Ltd

The book offers comprehensive content and includes industry best practices. Its unique coverage of data control, validation, and serialisation techniques for modern, data-driven digital design solutions makes it an indispensable and up-to-date reference guide.

Albert Hui MSc

A clear and practical guide that bridges user needs, technical design and system security. This book offers actionable insights for building thoughtful, resilient and user-centred digital solutions.

Harpal Lidder, VP, IIBA Toronto and Business Analyst,
MiWay, City of Mississauga

I highly recommend this book for its wealth of resources for business analysts looking to enrich their requirements analysis skills, adding depth to their thinking by considering a more holistic view of designing digital solutions.

Daniela Polito-Horton, Senior Business Analyst

Designing Digital Solutions offers a clear, practical overview of key design aspects like data, processes and security, equipping readers with best practices for effective digital solution design.

Joris Schut CISA CBAB CGEIT, Business Advisor, BearingPoint

An insightful and well-structured book that provides a comprehensive approach to creating user-centric digital experiences. Whether you're new to digital design or an experienced professional, this book is a must-read for refining your approach to solution-oriented design.

Bianca Christian, *Business Analyst,*
Young Business Analysts (YBA)

DESIGNING DIGITAL SOLUTIONS

BCS, THE CHARTERED INSTITUTE FOR IT

BCS, The Chartered Institute for IT, is committed to making IT good for society. We use the power of our network to bring about positive, tangible change. We champion the global IT profession and the interests of individuals, engaged in that profession, for the benefit of all.

Exchanging IT expertise and knowledge
The Institute fosters links between experts from industry, academia and business to promote new thinking, education and knowledge sharing.

Supporting practitioners
Through continuing professional development and a series of respected IT qualifications, the Institute seeks to promote professional practice tuned to the demands of business. It provides practical support and information services to its members and volunteer communities around the world.

Setting standards and frameworks
The Institute collaborates with government, industry and relevant bodies to establish good working practices, codes of conduct, skills frameworks and common standards. It also offers a range of consultancy services to employers to help them adopt best practice.

Become a member
Over 70,000 people including students, teachers, professionals and practitioners enjoy the benefits of BCS membership. These include access to an international community, invitations to a roster of local and national events, career development tools and a quarterly thought-leadership magazine. Visit www.bcs.org to find out more.

Further information
BCS, The Chartered Institute for IT,
3 Newbridge Square,
Swindon, SN1 1BY, United Kingdom.
T +44 (0) 1793 417 417
(Monday to Friday, 09:00 to 17:00 UK time)
bcs.org/contact

shop.bcs.org/
publishing@bcs.uk

bcs.org/qualifications-and-certifications/certifications-for-professionals/

DESIGNING DIGITAL SOLUTIONS
Architecting user experiences, processes, data and security

Peter Thompson

Published by BCS Learning and Development Ltd, a wholly owned subsidiary of BCS, The Chartered Institute for IT, 3 Newbridge Square, Swindon, SN1 1BY, UK.
www.bcs.org

EU GPSR Authorised Representative: LOGOS EUROPE, 9 Rue Nicolas Poussin, 17000 La Rochelle, France.
Contact@logoseurope.eu

Paperback ISBN: 978-1-78017-7083
PDF ISBN: 978-1-78017-7090
ePUB ISBN: 978-1-78017-7106

British Cataloguing in Publication Data.
A CIP catalogue record for this book is available at the British Library.

Publisher's acknowledgements
Reviewers: Holly Cummins, Amanda Chessell, Catherine Plumridge, Maria Papastashi
Publisher: Ian Borthwick
Commissioning editor: Heather Wood
Production manager: Florence Leroy
Project manager: Sunrise Setting Ltd
Copy-editor: Gary Smith
Proofreader: Barbara Eastman
Indexer: David Gaskell
Cover design: Alex Wright
Cover image: iStock/chunyip wong
Sales director: Charles Rumball
Typeset by Lapiz Digital Services, Chennai, India

CONTENTS

LIST OF FIGURES AND TABLES

ABOUT THE AUTHOR

Peter Thompson, having graduated from Leicester Polytechnic (now De Montfort University) in 1988 with a bachelor's degree in computer science, has amassed over 35 years' experience working in a variety of business change and solution development roles, including junior programmer, project manager, information systems consultant, systems development manager and managing director of an independent software house. His experience spans a diverse range of industries working with clients from broadcasting, utilities, logistics, financial services, commodities trading, food service, recruitment and leisure hire.

A Fellow of BCS, The Chartered Institute for IT, Peter is currently Learning Services Director at Assist Knowledge Development Ltd, an external examiner for the BCS International Diploma in Business Analysis, chief examiner for the BCS International Diploma in Solution Development and a member of the Leadership Panel for the BCS Business Systems Development certification schemes. He specialises in best practice techniques and standards in business analysis, data analysis and Agile software development, subjects that he continues to teach and practise today.

FOREWORD

Like many, I have a toolbox at home with a variety of tools that I pull out of the cupboard when there's a job to be done. Some of those tools are recent acquisitions, modern tools made of modern materials ideal for specific tasks. Some of the tools, however, have been in my toolbox far longer, with some even being tools I inherited from my father's toolbox. Some of those older tools still get used regularly as over the decades no-one, even with the benefit of modern manufacturing processes and recently developed materials, has managed to come up with a better version. Sometimes you think you've found a new tool, but when you look a bit closer you recognise an older tool slightly repurposed for the modern age, maybe powered-up with new technology.

I must admit there are some older tools which rarely get a look in, but every now and then you're thankful that you do have that obscure tool that is just right for the job, often for a job that the original manufacturer, or my father, could have never even imagined or foreseen.

I feel the same about my software modelling and development toolkit that has been slowly added to over the decades. There are a constant stream of new tools and techniques on offer, with supposedly better approaches towards using new and evolving technologies, patterns and architectures which let us develop systems in ways unimaginable twenty or thirty years ago. Adding these to my toolbox support new fresh ways of working, but on closer inspection many of these tools and techniques look familiar, repurposed for the new age (maybe powered-up with a sprinkling of AI). But there are many occasions when the ideal tool for the job may be a well-practised, old friend. For example, there is a reason that the most commonly used entity relationship diagramming syntax is still from Information Engineering (Crowsfoot) developed by Finkelstein and Martin in the 1970s.

In this series of books, the author reminds us that at a fundamental, essential level not a lot has changed; we still need to be able to perform analysis, architecture, design, build and testing. Only now we have a wider range of tools and techniques to select from, many of which are introduced across these books. New entrants into this field will find a useful catalogue to browse and consider. For more experienced practitioners, some items may already be in your personal toolbox, some you may have passed by thinking they're out-dated and irrelevant, but bear in mind that one day you may find yourself in need of one of them. Hopefully these books will provide a place to turn to refer you to the ideal tool whatever age it may be.

Julian Cox
April 2025

ACKNOWLEDGEMENTS

As is the case with many books, this book owes its existence to many individuals who have helped shape the final product.

First, a special thanks to James Cadle, who conceived, co-authored and edited the predecessor of this series (*Developing Information Systems: Practical Guidance for IT Professionals*). Without his early support and contribution, this book and its siblings (*Defining Digital Solutions* and *Delivering Digital Solutions*) would not have been possible.

I would also like to extend my gratitude to my wife, Sue, whose patience during many long hours of writing during evenings, weekends and holidays is laudable. I would also like to thank my step-daughter, Sophie, for her encouragement and support throughout this project, and special thanks to my son, Alex Bradley-Thompson, who contributed his extensive knowledge of data analytics and business intelligence, as well as acting as a sounding board and generally being there to empathise with the challenges of long hours writing and rewriting.

My colleagues at AssistKD have been hugely supportive during the writing of this book, and have contributed through many discussions on a variety of topics. In particular, Julian Cox (who also kindly provided the Foreword) and Debra Paul, who have meticulously reviewed various chapters and provided incredibly helpful feedback, and Megan Sullivan, who has produced some great images to illustrate some of the chapters.

Finally, this book could not have been produced without the professional publishing know-how of Ian Borthwick and Heather Wood from BCS – their patience and flexibility, as numerous deadlines have been pushed back due to other work commitments, is exemplary. I have benefited greatly from their expert advice.

ABBREVIATIONS

0NF	*See UNF*
1NF	*See FNF*
2NF	*See SNF*
3NF	*See TNF*
AAC	augmentative and alternative communication
ACID	atomic, consistent, isolated and durable
AES	Advanced Encryption Standard
AI	artificial intelligence
API	application programming interface
AR	augmented reality
AWS	Amazon Web Services
BA	business analyst
BCI	brain–computer interface
BDD	behaviour-driven development
BI	business intelligence
BPM	business process model
BPMN	business process model and notation
BRD	Business Requirements Document
BSOD	blue screen of death
CAD	computer-aided design
CASE	computer-aided software engineering
CBA	component-based architecture
CBD	component-based design
CCPA	California Consumer Privacy Act
CD	compact disc/continuous delivery/continuous deployment
CI	continuous integration
CIA	confidentiality, integrity, availability (CIA triad)
CIM	computer-independent model
CLI	command line interface
COTS	commercial off-the-shelf

CPRA	California Privacy Rights Act
CPU	central processing unit
CRC	cyclic redundancy check
CRM	customer relationship management
CSA	client–server architecture
CSF	Cybersecurity Framework
CSS	cascading style sheet
DAMA	Data Management Association
DBMS	database management system
DDD	domain-driven design
DDoS	distributed denial of service
DevOps	development operations
DFD	data flow diagram
DLP	data loss prevention
DLT	distributed ledger technology
DND	data navigation diagram
DoS	denial of service
DPA	Data Protection Act
DR	disaster recovery
DRY	don't repeat yourself
DVD	digital video disc
EA	enterprise architecture
EDA	event-driven architecture
ERD	entity–relationship diagram
ERP	enterprise resource planning
ESB	enterprise service bus
ETL	extract, transform, load
FIXML	Financial Information eXchange Markup Language
FNF	first normal form
FpML	Financial products Markup Language
GDPR	General Data Protection Regulation
GenAI	generative artificial intelligence
GIGO	garbage in, garbage out
GPS	Global Positioning System
GPT	Generative Pre-trained Transformer
gRPC	Google Remote Procedure Call
GSM	Global System for Mobile communication
GUI	graphical user interface
HA	high availability

HCD	human-centred design
HD	high definition
HDFS	Hadoop Distributed File System
HDR	high dynamic range
HIPS	host-based intrusion protection system
HTML	HyperText Markup Language
HTTP	HyperText Transfer Protocol
HTTPS	HyperText Transfer Protocol Secure
HUD	head-up display
I/O	input/output
IaaS	infrastructure as a service
IaC	infrastructure as code
ICT	information and communication technology
IDE	integrated development environment
IEEE	Institute of Electrical and Electronics Engineers
IoT	Internet of Things
IP	intellectual property/Internet Protocol
IPS	intrusion protection system
ISTQB	International Software Testing Qualifications Board
IT	information technology
ITM	IT manager
ITSM	IT service management
JSON	JavaScript Object Notation
KPI	key performance indicator
LCD	liquid crystal display
LED	light emitting diode
LLM	large language model
MDA	model-driven architecture
MDM	master data management
MFA	multifactor authentication
MICR	magnetic ink character recognition
ML	machine learning
MMS	Multimedia Messaging Service
MVC	model view controller
MVCC	multi-version concurrency control
MVVM	model view viewmodel
NCSC	National Cyber Security Centre
NFR	non-functional requirement
NIPS	network-based intrusion protection system

NIST	National Institute of Standards and Technology
NLP	natural language processing
NoSQL	Not Only SQL (*see also SQL*)
NUI	natural user interface
OCR	optical character recognition
OLAP	online analytical processing
OLED	organic light emitting diode
OLTP	online transaction processing
OMG	Object Management Group
OMR	optical mark recognition
ONIX	ONline Information eXchange
On-Prem	on premises
ORM	object-relational mapping
OSI	Open Systems Interconnect
OWASP	Open Web Application Security Project
PaaS	platform as a service
PII	personal identifiable information
PIM	platform-independent model
PoLP	principle of least privilege
POPIT	People, Organisation, Processes, Information and Technology
PPM	pages per minute
ProtoBuf	protocol buffers
PSM	platform-specific model
QR	quick response
RBAC	role-based access control
RDA	relational data analysis
RDBMS	Relational Database Management System
RE	Requirements Engineering
REST	Representational State Transfer
RFID	radio frequency identification
SaaS	software as a service
SAR	subject access request
SDLC	software development life cycle
SLA	service-level agreement
SME	subject-matter expert
SMS	Short Message Service
SNF	second normal form
SOA	service-oriented architecture
SOAP	Simple Object Access Protocol

SOD	service-oriented design
SQL	Structured Query Language
SRP	single responsibility principle
SSID	service set identifier
SVG	scalable vector graphics
SWOT	strengths, weaknesses, opportunities, threats
SysML	Systems Modeling Language
TCP/IP	Transmission Control Protocol/Internet Protocol
TDD	test-driven development
TLS	Transport Layer Security
TNF	third normal form
TOGAF	The Open Group Architecture Framework
TTS	text to speech
UCD	user-centred design
UDDI	universal description, discovery and integration
UDL	Unified Database Language
UDP	User Datagram Protocol
UHD	ultra-high definition
UI	user interface
UML	Unified Modeling Language
UNF	un-normalised form
URL	uniform resource locator
USB	Universal Serial Bus
UWF	Universal Windows Platform
UX	user experience
VR	virtual reality
VUI	voice user interface
W3C	World Wide Web Consortium
WAI	Web Accessibility Initiative
WCAG	Web Content Accessibility Guidelines
WIMP	Windows, Icons, Menus, Pointing device
WPF	Windows Presentation Foundation
WSDL	Web Services Description Language
XML	eXtensible Markup Language
XP	eXtreme Programming
XSS	cross-site scripting
YAML	Yet Another Markup Language

PREFACE

Digital solutions have revolutionised our everyday lives. Everything we touch and do these days – ordering products and services, booking our next holiday, reading, listening to music, watching a movie, driving a car, telling the time, calling or messaging a friend, colleague or loved one – will have a digital solution at work somewhere. The ever-evolving technological landscape has transformed how organisations solve problems, streamline operations and drive innovation.

This book, the second instalment in a three-part series, continues the exploration of the digital solution life cycle (introduced in Book 1, *Defining Digital Solutions*, and reproduced in Figure 0.1). It provides an in-depth examination of the principles, methodologies, techniques and technologies essential for effective digital solution design, bridging the gap between business requirements (the focus of Book 1) and technological execution (the focus of Book 3, *Delivering Digital Solutions*). By doing so, it equips business change and information technology (IT) professionals with the tools needed to create scalable, user-centred digital solutions that offer real value to the organisations who procure them and the customers who use them.

Figure 0.1 Life cycle of a digital solution

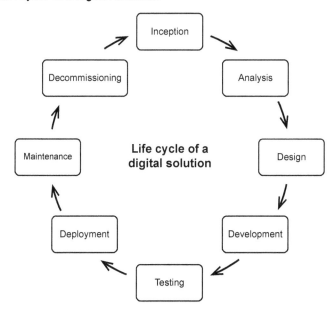

The journey begins by defining the practice of digital solution design, highlighting its objectives, constraints and vital role in aligning technology with organisational goals. The book then explores design paradigms, such as monolithic, component-based and service-oriented, shedding light on their strengths and practical applications. User-centricity lies at the heart of modern solutions, and Chapter 3 initiates the design process by delving into input, output and user interface (UI) design, with a focus on ensuring solutions address user needs while employing the right technologies for their specific context of use.

Chapters 4–6 complete the design process by exploring digital process design, showcasing techniques to optimise workflows, improve efficiency and balance cohesion and flexibility within software solutions. The design process continues with the design of data structures for persistent data storage and for data in transit, using popular data technologies and emphasising key concepts such as concurrency, scalability and security to build robust and reliable data structures. The final part of the design process considers system controls to safeguard solutions against vulnerabilities and to manage the risks associated with the use of digital solutions, recognising the critical importance of cybersecurity.

Chapter 7 delivers a detailed discussion on solution and software architecture, and how they relate to the more holistic discipline of enterprise architecture. Architectural principles, standards and patterns are discussed in the context of providing a structured framework for the design of a digital solution that ensures consistency, scalability, maintainability and alignment with business goals and technical requirements.

The book concludes by examining popular software tools that support digital solution design, offering a practical toolkit to promote collaboration, optimise workflows and speed up the design process. The final chapter provides a brief introduction to Book 3.

Written in an accessible style, this book combines practical advice with real-world examples to demonstrate best practices. Building on the foundation established in *Defining Digital Solutions*, this book demystifies the complex art of translating solution requirements into actionable blueprints for realising them.

Whether you are an experienced practitioner or new to the field, this book – and its companions in the series, *Defining Digital Solutions* and *Delivering Digital Solutions* – will empower you to actively contribute to the design, development and delivery of digital solutions that meet the demands of a dynamic, ever-evolving world. By embracing the concepts and frameworks outlined in these pages, you will be equipped to drive meaningful change and create lasting value through technology.

WHO IS THIS BOOK FOR?

When the idea for the Digital Solutions Collection was originally conceived, the following categories of reader were envisaged:

- **Business analysts (BAs)**: This book provides a comprehensive understanding of how digital solution design translates business requirements into actionable solutions.

- **Project managers and delivery managers**: This book provides valuable insights into design methodologies, principles, tools and the strategic application of digital technologies to ensure solutions meet business objectives while adhering to timelines and budgets. It emphasises the significance of collaboration between technical and business teams, effective risk management and best practices for creating scalable, user-centred solutions, empowering project managers to achieve successful outcomes in complex and dynamic projects.

- **Product managers**: This book examines how product features are brought to life through the effective application of technology, offering practical guidance to support the development of scalable, user-centric products. With a focus on collaboration between technical and business teams, as well as addressing risk management and best practices, the book equips product managers to prioritise features, engage effectively with stakeholders and deliver innovative, market-ready solutions that create measurable value.

- **IT managers (ITMs)**: This book offers guidance on leveraging digital technologies to implement and sustain solutions effectively, while managing associated risks, ensuring compliance with technical policies and legislation, and aligning with organisational goals.

- **Solution developers, testers and technical stakeholders**: This book provides a comprehensive understanding of the digital solution design process, bridging the gap between technical execution and business objectives. It offers practical guidance on design methodologies, principles and tools, enabling developers to build scalable, user-centric solutions and testers to ensure quality and reliability. For technical stakeholders, the book highlights best practices, risk management strategies and collaboration techniques, equipping them to contribute effectively to the development and delivery of robust and compliant digital solutions.

- **Business stakeholders**: This book outlines the methodologies, principles and tools required to transform business needs into impactful digital solutions, addressing key stakeholder priorities such as scalability, user satisfaction and return on investment. It also promotes stronger collaboration between business and technical teams, enabling stakeholders to make informed decisions and play an active role in the success of digital initiatives.

- **Students on university and other courses studying digital business change**: This book provides detailed guidance on how the requirements for a digital solution are translated into actionable blueprints for realising them, while employing the most appropriate technologies to meet the needs of the context for use, thereby making it essential reading for students in business analysis, IT, software development and digital transformation. With a focus on contemporary practices such as Agile, cloud solutions and collaborative tools, the book equips students with the skills needed to thrive in a rapidly evolving, innovation-driven industry while emphasising the strategic alignment of solutions with organisational goals.

- **Candidates studying for the BCS International Diploma in Solution Development**: This book provides a body of knowledge that covers the breadth of the diploma syllabus and also a range of associated certificates within the diploma scheme.

HOW TO USE THIS BOOK

This book can be used in a number of ways:

- It can be read from cover to cover to provide a good general understanding of the subject, especially for those with little previous exposure to the discipline of digital solution design.

- Each chapter also stands alone to provide a detailed reference guide to specific aspects of digital solution design, so the reader can choose to dip into the chapters in any order. However, it is recommended that Chapter 1 is read first to provide context for the remaining chapters.

- If more detail is desired after digesting the content of this book, readers can pursue specific topics via the references and further reading section.

Peter Thompson
February 2025

1   WHAT IS DIGITAL SOLUTION DESIGN?

INTRODUCTION

Writing about digital solution design presents a unique challenge because, unlike many other disciplines, it is constantly evolving. The foundational principles of design approaches are continually questioned as new technologies emerge and business challenges demand faster and more adaptable digital solutions. However, not all organisations operate at the forefront of technological innovation, with many still heavily investing in what could be considered legacy technologies and paradigms.

An additional challenge comes in understanding exactly what design is about. Cross (2006) provides a useful definition:

> Design refers to the process of creating a plan or solution to meet specific goals or requirements, often involving iterative problem-solving, creativity, and the consideration of constraints and user needs. It encompasses both the process and the outcome, balancing functionality, aesthetics, and practicality.

So, the term 'solution design' can be used to refer to both a deliverable (or set of deliverables) and the activity of producing the deliverable(s). There is also a more elusive side to design in terms of the creativity employed by the designer when deciding on the best way to achieve a desired outcome, which often comes down to the inherent abilities, sensibilities and values of individuals, and is difficult to define in words.

With the advent of Agile software development practices, design for many development teams has become lost as a professional discipline. Agile methodologies, such as Scrum or eXtreme Programming (XP), prioritise flexibility, iterative development and rapid delivery of functional software. While these principles have proven effective in many scenarios, they often lead to insufficient emphasis on up-front or explicit design, which can result in certain challenges.

Agile favours emergent design, where the architecture of the solution evolves iteratively alongside the development process. While this allows flexibility, it can lead to fragmented or inconsistent designs, especially in large-scale systems where long-term architectural considerations are critical. Additionally, without sufficient initial design, teams may implement quick fixes or short-term solutions that accumulate as technical debt. Over time, this can reduce the maintainability and scalability of the solution. To address these (and other) issues, many Agile teams adopt hybrid approaches, such as:

- **Lightweight up-front design**: Conducting minimal but critical design activities at the beginning of development to establish a foundational architecture.
- **Design reviews and retrospectives**: Regularly revisiting the design to ensure alignment with long-term goals.
- **Dedicated architecture iterations (Sprints)**: Allocating time for focused design or architectural planning during Sprints.

This chapter, and the next five, focus on the mechanics of solution design, considering the objectives, constraints, approaches, activities and techniques involved; the more artistic side of design is outside the scope of this book.

THE OBJECTIVES OF DESIGN

The primary objective of solution design is to determine how the proposed solution will realise the requirements identified during Requirements Engineering (RE). These requirements will typically be categorised as functional or non-functional and are predominantly defined from the perspective of the business stakeholders and end-users. However, the solution developers themselves will have their own requirements in terms of product quality. The **Product Quality Model** defined within ISO/IEC 25010:2023 (ISO, 2023a) is an international standard that describes nine product quality characteristics:

- **Functional suitability**: How well the software provides functions that meet stated and implied needs when used under specified conditions.
- **Performance efficiency**: The performance relative to the amount of resources used under stated conditions.
- **Compatibility**: The ability of the software to interact with other systems or products without conflict.
- **Interaction capability** (formerly known as usability): The effectiveness and satisfaction with which specified users achieve specified goals in particular environments.
- **Reliability**: The capability of the software to maintain a specified level of performance when used under specified conditions.
- **Security**: The protection of information and data to ensure that individuals or systems have the degree of data access appropriate to their types and levels of authorisation.
- **Maintainability**: The ease with which the software can be modified to correct faults, improve performance or other attributes, or adapt to a changed environment.
- **Flexibility** (previously referred to as portability): The ability of the software to be transferred from one environment to another.
- **Safety**: The ability of the software to protect against acceptable levels of risk of harm to people, business, software, property or the environment in a specified context of use.

A complementary standard, ISO/IEC 25019:2023 (ISO, 2023b) defines the **Quality in Use Model**, which describes three primary quality-in-use characteristics:

- **Effectiveness**: The accuracy and completeness with which users achieve specific goals in particular environments.
- **Efficiency**: The resources expended in relation to the accuracy and completeness of goals achieved.
- **Satisfaction**: The degree to which user needs are fulfilled when a product or system is used in a specified context.

Together, the Product Quality Model and Quality in Use Model provide a comprehensive framework for specifying, measuring, evaluating and improving the quality of information and communication technology (ICT) products and software, ensuring that systems and software meet stakeholder needs effectively and efficiently in their intended operational environments.

Table 1.1 combines these two sets of quality characteristics, which together with a set of typical business requirement categories, provides a clear set of objectives for solution design.

Table 1.1 Solution design objectives

Objective	Sub-objective
Realisation of functional requirements	• Functionally correct and complete
Realisation of non-functional requirements	• Usable (user-friendly) • Reliable • Secure • Accessible • Available • Capacity and throughput • Responsive • Flexible • Scalable • Portable • Configurable
Conformance with product design characteristics	• Maintainable • Modular • Extensible • Simple • Efficient • Reusable • Testable • Conformant • Compatible • Interoperable • Safe

Taking each objective in turn:

Functionally correct and complete	The design realises the functionality specified in functional requirements, including data maintenance, transactional processes (such as raise invoice, despatch order, renew policy), generation of reports and other outputs.
Usable (user-friendly)	Delivers the functional requirements in a consistent, intuitive way to achieve a positive experience for the intended users.
Reliable	Ensures that the solution is robust (not prone to failure) and available at all times when needed.
Secure	Provides adequate controls to restrict access to the solution and its data, often for the sake of commercial sensitivity or to satisfy privacy legislation and similar regulations.
Accessible	Ensures that the solution is accessible to all potential users regardless of the limitations of disability, their native language or other relevant considerations.
Available	Ensures that the solution is available when required to fulfil its purpose, often determined by business working hours. See also *reliable*.
Capacity	Supports transaction and data volumes as necessary to provide continuous operation into the foreseeable future.
Throughput	Similar to capacity, throughput relates to data/transactional volumes within a specific time frame, such as the ability to capture 1,000 orders per hour or to support 100,000 simultaneous accesses to a specific internet site.
Responsive	Ensures that the solution provides a response to a particular request within a predetermined time frame.
Flexible	The ability to adapt to changing business situations. This is a difficult objective to achieve, and is impossible to guarantee. The objectives of scalability, portability and configurability essentially break this objective down into more specific, testable solution features.
Scalable	The ability to up- or downscale the number of transactions and/or users to support changing business requirements.
Portable	The ability to translate the design to work using different technology platforms and devices.
Configurable	The ability to change the solution's behaviour by setting configuration options or defining system parameters.

Maintainable   The ability to fix defects and make changes to functionality, performance or usability after the solution is live. The objectives *simple* and *flexible* go some way to enabling maintainability, but good documentation is also important.

Modular   The design is based upon the principles of loose (or low) coupling and high cohesion. These concepts are explored later in this chapter.

Extensible   This is synonymous with *flexible*.

Simple   The design is not unnecessarily complex, as complexity can lead to code that is error-prone or difficult to maintain.

Efficient   This refers to how effectively the solution uses resources to achieve a desired outcome. There are numerous different facets to efficiency, including:

- **Algorithmic**: How quickly and simply a task can be accomplished.
- **Computational**: Optimal use of resources such as central processing unit (CPU) time, memory, network bandwidth and data storage.
- **Data**: Optimal storage and retrieval of data.
- **Energy**: The solution consumes less power, leading to longer battery life or reduced energy costs.
- **Usability**: Ensuring that tasks can be completed with minimal steps, confusion or unnecessary complications.
- **Scalability**: If the user base or data volume grows, the solution should still perform optimally without requiring redesign.
- **Security**: Effective security measures prevent resource-intensive attacks and minimise the overhead associated with securing access to the solution and its data.
- **Cost efficiency**: The solution delivers the desired results at the lowest cost, considering both initial development and ongoing maintenance costs.

Reusable   The design makes use of existing functionality, where available. This may take the form of generic functions, components or services provided by third-party providers, or standardised functions, components and services developed in-house.

Testable   The design is expressed in a way that enables software testers to easily develop test cases and scripts directly from the design deliverables (artefacts).

Conformant   The design adheres to standards such as modelling notation and industry-wide user interface (UI) and software engineering standards, as well as complying with architectural principles and policies, such as modularity and simplicity.

Compatible   Use of standard data file or message formats (protocols) that enable interoperability (see below) and data sharing with other solutions. For example, many independent software products provide the ability to read and/or generate files that can be used by Microsoft Office applications.

Interoperable   The ability to work (operate) with other systems. In practice this may refer to the ability for a solution to share data with another solution or to consume services provided by another solution.

Safe   The design mitigates the risk of harm to people, business, software, property or the environment in a specified context of use.

In addition to these overarching objectives, individual design activities (e.g. input design) have their own objectives, which shall be covered when considering the scope of digital solution design later in this chapter.

CONSTRAINTS AFFECTING THE DESIGN

While striving to achieve the above objectives, the solution designer has a number of constraints placed upon their work. Some common constraints are shown in Table 1.2.

Table 1.2 Common constraints affecting solution design

Type of constraint	Constraint
Project constraints	• Budget • Timescale • Resources • Skills • Standards
Technical constraints	• Hardware • Software • Legacy solutions • Programming language • Standards
Organisational constraints	• Stakeholders • Legislation and regulations • Cultural differences • Quality of requirements • Standards

Project constraints represent limitations imposed by project stakeholders and are agreed during project initiation. Technical constraints are also identified during project initiation but, unlike project constraints, they tend to relate to more strategic issues often defined within enterprise-wide IT architecture policies, standards and principles that govern a range of – or all – projects.

The development organisation, or even the customer organisation if the developers are a third-party provider, often imposes constraints that must be adhered to by the designer. Some of these relate to technical standards, shown in Table 1.2 under technical constraints.

Taking each constraint in turn:

Budget   It is very rare for a project to proceed without a predefined budget. With digital solution development projects, the budget may restrict the scope of features that can be delivered. This may also lead to trade-offs between design objectives. For example, reusability, scalability and efficiency may be desirable objectives, but it is often more costly to build software in such a way that these are achieved.

Timescale   Deadlines and target dates generally impose similar restrictions to budget as the two are intricately linked.

Resources   Projects rarely have unlimited resources at their disposal. This is often
and skills   a direct consequence of a limited budget, but may also be due to the availability of other resources. Person-based restrictions often have the greatest impact on the design stage of development, in terms of a lack of skills in a particular technology, although a lack of access to the latest technology (in terms of hardware and software) may also be a constraining factor. These factors often steer the design of a system down the tried-and-tested path that an organisation is familiar with rather than breaking new ground.

Standards   Standards can impose constraints at all levels (project, technical and organisational). Project standards can be determined by organisational standards and can dictate the modelling language to be used (e.g. the Unified Modeling Language, or UML), documentation formats and methodology. Technical standards may include:

- **UI style guides** such as those defined by Apple and Microsoft and the Web Content Accessibility Guidelines (WCAG) defined by the World Wide Web Consortium (W3C, 2018);
- **data formats** such as the use of open standards (e.g. XML);
- **protocols** such as Simple Object Access Protocol (SOAP) and Representational State Transfer (REST), used for passing messages in a service-oriented architecture;
- **security** such as ISO 27001 (ISO, 2013), ISO/IEC 7498 (ISO, 1994), ISO/IEC 13335 (ISO, 2004), ISO/IEC 27005 (ISO, 2022a);

- **AI standards** such as the European Commission's *Ethics Guidelines for Trustworthy AI* (European Commission, 2019) and its *Ethics by Design and Ethics of Use Approaches for AI* (European Commission, 2021), and ISO/IEC 22989 (ISO, 2022b) and ISO/IEC 23053 (ISO, 2022c), which establishes a framework for AI systems using machine learning; and

- **application-specific standards** such as Payment Card Industry Data Security Standard (PCI DSS) (PCI Security Standards Council, 2022).

Some organisations define their own standards in addition to industry-wide standards adopted for achieving best practice. Some typical examples of organisation-specific standards include:

- **UI style guides** prescribing such things as consistent use of fonts and corporate colours, positioning of logos and use of standard terminology;

- **reporting standards** that are similar to user interface guidelines, but govern the look and feel, layout, sorting, filtering and totalling on reports generated by digital solutions; and

- **module design guidelines**, where some organisations define standards that must be met during process design regarding the coupling, cohesion and simplicity of software processes and components.

Hardware and software	Organisational standards may dictate that only certain hardware or software will be used, often a consequence of an enterprise-wide contract with certain vendors. This is especially true of organisations that have introduced enterprise architecture teams to define and govern the use of IT.
Legacy solutions	If the solution under development needs to interface to legacy solutions (those built using older technologies that the organisation no longer uses for new developments), then the solution design may need to use specific protocols or file formats that are no longer in general use, some of which may no longer be supported. This may require proprietary development languages to develop interfaces with the legacy systems. The adapter design pattern (also referred to as a 'wrapper') that translates between old and new formats and protocols is often used to simplify interfaces with legacy technologies (see Chapter 2).
Programming language	Organisations often have enterprise-wide standards regarding the programming languages and development tools to be used during digital solution development. This may constrain the designer as not all languages provide the same features. Additionally, legacy languages, such as COBOL and Visual Basic, do not provide support for some design paradigms, such as service-oriented design (see Chapter 2).

| Stakeholders | There are typically three key issues relating to stakeholders that constrain the designer's ability to complete their work: |

- **Availability**: Perhaps the greatest constraining factor regarding stakeholders is their availability for providing clarification regarding their requirements. Even accepting that the requirements provided to the designer are of good quality, they often change during the development process.

- **Authority**: Sometimes the ability to obtain authorisation for changes is restricted due to the stakeholders requesting them having insufficient authority.

- **Sign-off**: The ability of stakeholders to approve and sign-off the design before software construction commences is highly questionable in many system development projects, mainly down to the use of esoteric notations and models during the design process. Consequently, design specifications are rarely approved and signed off by business stakeholders.

| Legislation and regulations | Arguably the most prevalent legislation affecting digital solutions is data protection legislation, such as the UK Data Protection Act 2018 (DPA; UK Government, 2018). However, each industry sector has its own legislation to contend with, which typically places restrictions on the designer, who needs to ensure compliance within the solution. |

| Cultural differences | Often, digital solutions need to work in different environments and different countries, which have different ways of working, different languages and different currencies. This may restrict the way a solution is designed or may require a particular approach that conflicts with design objectives such as simplicity and maintainability. |

| Quality of requirements | Perhaps the factor most attributed to the failure (or success) of a solution development project is the quality of requirements. Requirements Engineering (explored in Book 1, *Defining Digital Solutions*) strives to produce high-quality, fit-for-purpose requirements, but unfortunately it is still commonplace to see requirements that do not meet such stringent quality criteria. This leaves some solution features open to interpretation, which, ultimately, requires more of the designer's time seeking clarification, or worse, having to re-work the design later in the development life cycle, or when the solution is in live operational use – often at significant cost. |

THE SCOPE OF DIGITAL SOLUTION DESIGN

Although each digital solution development project is different, a good place to start when considering the scope of design is to identify the key elements of a digital solution, as shown in Figure 1.1.

Figure 1.1 Key elements of a digital solution

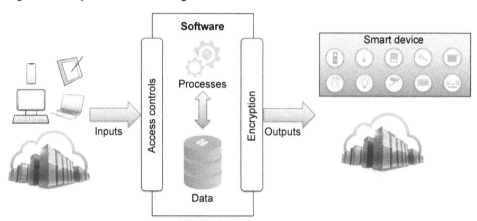

The four key elements identified in Figure 1.1 are: inputs, outputs, processes and data. However, there is a fifth element that impacts all four: security and system controls, such as access controls, verification, validation and encryption. Therefore, the key activities of digital solution design can be summarised as:

- **Input and output (I/O) design**: The identification and design of inputs and outputs for digital solutions, based on the requirements captured during Requirements Engineering. A critical aspect of I/O design is the selection of appropriate technologies for inputs (e.g. keyboards, voice recognition and biometric scanners) and outputs (e.g. monitors, printers and Braille displays). As inputs and outputs often involve interactions between a digital solution and human users, I/O design typically incorporates the design of the user experience, and more specifically the UI.

- **Process design**: Focuses on defining and refining workflows within digital solutions. During process design the designer uses design principles such as coupling, cohesion and stepwise refinement to optimise software processes for efficiency, reliability and maintainability. Process design necessitates balancing design principles with constraints such as resources, scalability and organisational needs to ensure alignment with functional and non-functional requirements.

- **Data design**: Involves the design of data structures and how they are managed within the digital solution. The designer may use techniques such as normalisation or dimensional modelling to optimise the data structures to best suit the processing needs of the solution, while also ensuring concurrency, scalability and efficient data retrieval. As with all aspects of design, the designer must consider the implications of technological constraints and data security to ensure system performance and reliability.

- **Security and control design**: Encompasses the design of cybersecurity features and system controls aimed at mitigating or preventing risks associated with digital solutions. It also ensures compliance with external legislation, regulations and internal organisational policies and business rules. Designers must address potential vulnerabilities that could lead to software failures or cyberattacks. Rather than being a standalone task, the design of system controls is inherently integrated into all other aspects of digital solution design.

These individual design activities are explored further in Chapters 3–6.

2   APPROACHES TO DIGITAL SOLUTION DESIGN

INTRODUCTION

A given approach to solution design, more formally referred to as a software design paradigm, encompasses a set of principles, practices and patterns that help designers to specify solutions that meet many, if not all, of the design objectives introduced in Chapter 1.

It is almost impossible when discussing software design not to consider software architecture, which is explored in Chapter 7. Many of the software design paradigms can also be seen as patterns of software architecture.

This chapter provides a brief introduction to the most popular design paradigms (monolithic design, component-based design, service-oriented design and domain-driven design), and also explains the distinction between logical and physical design. It concludes with a brief introduction to design patterns, which are explored further in later chapters.

MONOLITHIC DESIGN

With a monolithic approach to design, all components of a software application are tightly coupled (see below) and operate as a single, unified unit. In this approach, the entire application is built and deployed as a single cohesive entity, with all functions – such as user interfaces, business logic and data access – residing in a single codebase or executable.

Monolithic design exhibits the following key characteristics:

- **Single codebase**: The application is developed and maintained as a single collection of source code, including all files, scripts, libraries and resources necessary for development, maintenance and deployment.
- **Tight coupling**: Components are interdependent, meaning changes to one part of the codebase often affect other parts. Coupling is explored further in Chapters 4 and 7.
- **Centralised deployment**: The entire application is packaged and deployed together, typically as one executable or server instance.

- **Unified technology stack**: The entire system generally uses a single programming language or technology stack.

Although monolithic design has been largely superseded by component-based and service-oriented design, it does offer several advantages:

- **Simplicity**: It is straightforward to develop and deploy, especially for smaller applications.
- **Straightforward development environment**: Developers work in a unified environment with fewer moving parts, reducing the complexity of coordination.
- **Performance**: Communication between components is internal, often leading to faster execution compared to distributed systems.
- **Lower initial costs**: Fewer tools, frameworks and infrastructure are needed to get started.

However, it is the disadvantages associated with monolithic design that have led to the adoption of component-based and service-oriented design:

- **Scalability issues**: Scaling specific parts of the application independently is challenging; the entire system must be scaled together.
- **Maintenance complexity**: As the application grows, the codebase can become large and unwieldy, making updates and debugging difficult.
- **Risk of downtime**: Since all components are interdependent, a failure in one part can bring down the entire system.
- **Limited flexibility**: The tight coupling and unified technology stack make it difficult to adopt new technologies or methodologies for specific parts of the application.

While monolithic design is typically associated with legacy systems, it can be suitable for small applications (such as those developed by startups or small-scale projects) due to its simplicity and cost-effectiveness. An example of monolithic design is included in Chapter 4.

COMPONENT-BASED DESIGN

Component-based design (CBD) emerged from the need to create more robust and reliable software solutions in a more efficient manner. It addresses the limitations of earlier monolithic solutions, which were prone to frequent crashes and failures, often caused by tight coupling, as well as the long development times required to deliver working solutions. CBD promotes the assembly of software applications from components sourced from various origins, with the components potentially written in multiple programming languages and capable of running on different platforms.

CBD exhibits the following key characteristics:

- **Modularity**: Components are independent building blocks that can be developed, tested and deployed separately.

- **Reusability**: Components are designed to be reused across different applications, reducing duplication of effort and increasing standardisation.

- **Interoperability**: Components interact with one another via standardised interfaces, ensuring seamless communication regardless of their origin or underlying technology.

- **Platform independence**: Components may be written in different programming languages and run on various platforms.

Many industries today, from electronics to car manufacture, are based around the assembly of products from standardised components. In the case of software engineering, this offers several benefits:

- **Faster development**: Leveraging pre-built components accelerates the development process.

- **Improved quality**: Components are often well-tested and proven in other applications, leading to more reliable solutions.

- **Cost efficiency**: Reusing components reduces development costs by minimising the need for redundant coding.

- **Ease of maintenance**: Modular components make it easier to identify and fix issues without impacting the entire system.

- **Flexibility**: New features can be added by integrating additional components without major system overhauls.

- **Scalability**: Components can be replaced relatively easily with newer versions that use more scalable technologies.

CBD is commonly used in the following types of digital solution:

- **Web applications**: Frameworks such as React and Angular use CBD principles to create reusable UI elements.

- **Enterprise systems**: Applications such as enterprise resource planning (ERP) and customer relationship management (CRM) often consist of modular components for specific business processes.

- **Embedded systems**: In devices such as IoT (Internet of Things) sensors or automotive systems, CBD allows efficient design of specialised functionality.

Components are the fundamental building blocks that can be assembled into a solution. When defining the components that make up a digital solution, the designer must consider the following elements:

- **Role**: The purpose of the component within the solution.

- **Responsibilities**: Specific responsibilities to fulfil the role. With regard to software, these include UI management, business logic, process flow control and data management responsibilities.

- **Services**: The set of self-contained units of functionality that a component can provide to other components through one or more interfaces.

- **Interfaces**: The means by which other components may access the component's services.

- **Dependencies**: Services provided by other components that the component requires to enable it to provide its own services.

What is common to most definitions of 'software component' is the notion that a component has an inside and an outside, and a relationship between the two. The inside of a software component is a discrete piece of software realising certain responsibilities. It is a device, artefact or asset that can be managed to achieve reuse. The outside of a software component is an interface that exposes a set of services that the component provides to other components.

Components can exist independently of each other, but can also be assembled together to build new solutions; they provide services to other components and use services provided by other components, as shown in the UML component diagram in Figure 2.1.

Figure 2.1 Integrated components in a sales order processing solution

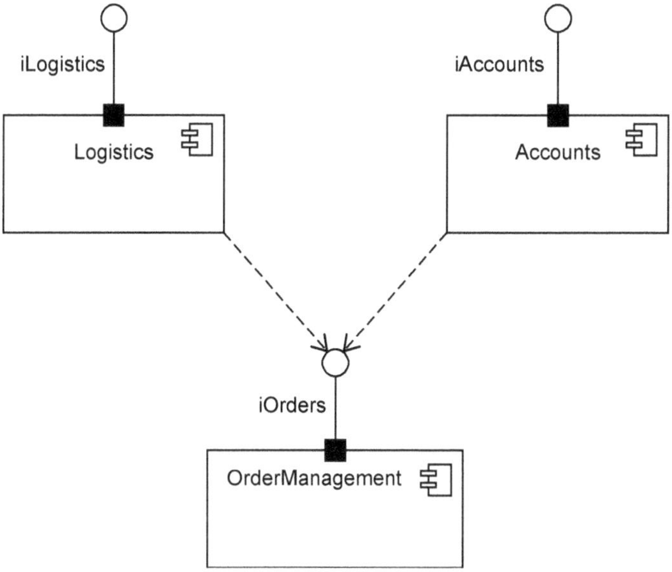

Figure 2.1 shows three components (Logistics, Accounts and OrderManagement) that make up a sales order processing solution. The Logistics component exposes an interface (commonly referred to as an API, or application programming interface) called iLogistics that can be used by other components to consume the services that it provides. Similarly, the Accounts component exposes an interface called iAccounts and the OrderManagement component exposes an interface called iOrders. Figure 2.1 also shows that the Logistics and Accounts components are both using services provided by the OrderManagement component, by virtue of the fact that they have dependencies on the iOrders interface (shown as dashed arrows).

Figure 2.2 shows the definition of the iOrders interface using UML class diagram notation.

Figure 2.2 Definition of the iOrders interface

<<interface>>
iOrders
+ getOrderDetails(orderNo) :xml
+ checkOrderStatus(orderNo) :char
+ pickOrder(orderNo, pickDate) :void
+ despatchOrder(orderNo, despatchDate) :void
+ confirmDelivery(orderNo, deliveryDate) :void
+ cancelOrder(orderNo, dateCancelled) :boolean

The interface in Figure 2.2 shows the discrete services (e.g. getOrderDetails) that can be invoked by other components, along with a definition of the message format that must be used to invoke each service, and any return values provided by the OrderManagement component. For example, any component invoking the getOrderDetails service must provide the order number to uniquely identify the order that they require the details for, and, in turn, the OrderManagement component will return an XML data structure containing the required details.

Components exist at varying levels of granularity. Some are defined at a very low level and serve as fundamental building blocks for widespread reuse across diverse digital solution development projects. For instance, software houses maintain extensive internal inventories of documented and tested components that developers leverage to build applications, while modern operating systems include comprehensive libraries of built-in components that facilitate standard application functionality. Conversely, other components function as fully encapsulated applications, capable of integration with other application-level components to form more extensive solutions.

As granularity increases, it is likely that components will be purchased externally and implemented into the application software. External purchase of components requires a clear understanding of the role of the components within the overall solution, the services the components provide, and the services they require to provide those services. Small, more finely grained components may also be purchased, and these find their way into many applications. Some components are open source and may be modified to suit the specific needs of the overall solution, while others are closed and the program code inside the component is not accessible or visible to the solution developer. In some situations, entire off-the-shelf products (discussed in *Defining Digital Solutions*) become components within the context of a broader, multi-application solution. This is common with ERP solutions.

When performing CBD, the designer determines the most effective way to spread the functionality needed to realise the solution requirements across a set of components.

This requires skill, knowledge and experience of both the available technologies and the application domain, to maximise the potential for reusing existing components, and, where new components are required, the potential to share the new component services in the future. The designer must also ensure that their final design achieves the relevant objectives identified in Chapter 1.

Figure 2.3 shows a UML deployment diagram that highlights how a series of discrete components can be assembled to form a solution across a range of disparate devices.

Figure 2.3 UML deployment diagram showing a component-based solution

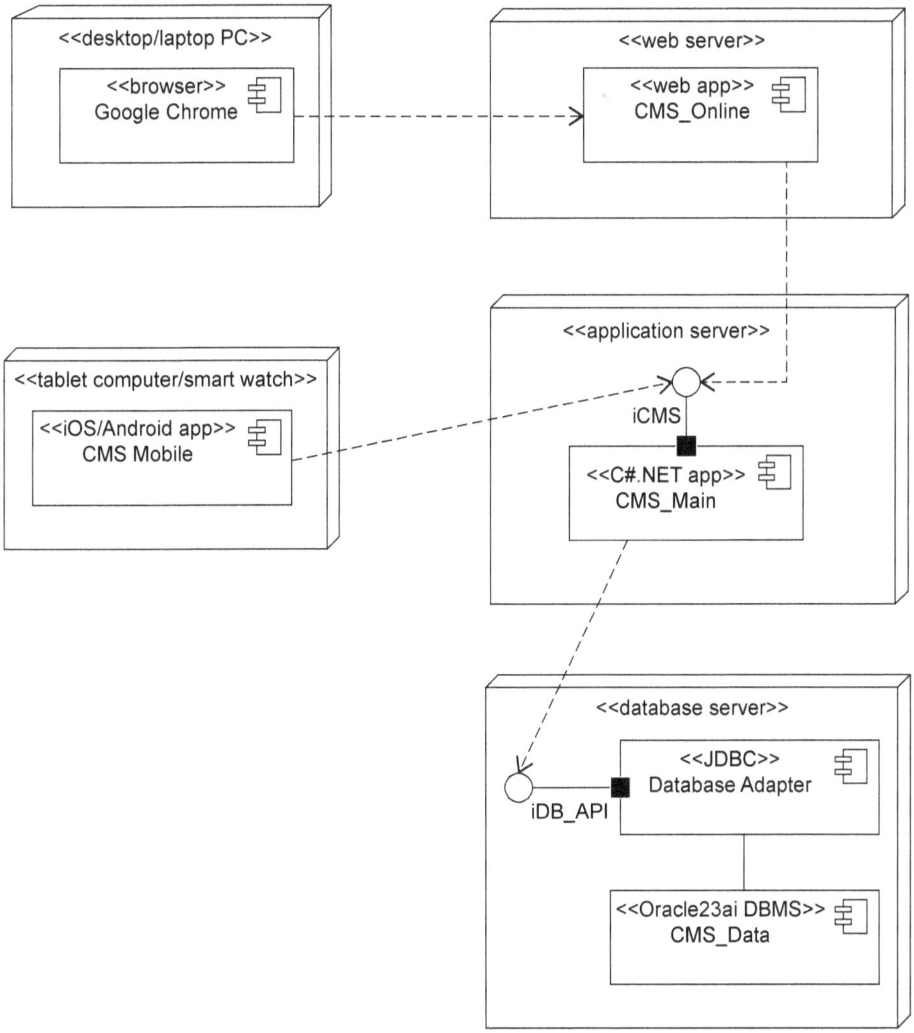

The three dimensional cubes in Figure 2.3 are referred to as nodes in UML, which represent devices within the solution infrastructure. UML stereotypes («...») are used to further clarify the roles of each device («`web server`», «`application server`», «`database server`») and also the different types of component or technology used («`browser`», «`iOS/Android app`», «`Web app`», «`C#.NET app`», «`Oracle 23ai DBMS`», «`JDBC`»).

An example of CBD is included in Chapter 4.

SERVICE-ORIENTED DESIGN

In the context of digital solutions, a 'service' refers to a self-contained, modular unit of functionality offered by a software component or application, typically accessible through a well-defined interface. Service-oriented design (SOD), often synonymous with service-oriented architecture (SOA), focuses on assembling a collection of software services to create a digital solution that addresses the requirements of a customer or end-user. This approach involves building the solution from distinct, loosely coupled and reusable services that communicate over a network, which can be within a local environment or distributed across the internet. Each service represents a specific business function or capability and is designed to be independently developed, deployed and managed.

A SOD/SOA comprises the following elements:

- **Service provider**: Hosts and offers specific functionality (services) that can be consumed by service consumers. The service provider implements the logic that realises the functionality or capability that the service provides, registers the service with the service registry and responds to requests from the service consumer. A typical example of a service provider is a payment gateway API that handles transactions from merchant systems.

- **Service consumer**: An application, user or system that requests and uses services provided by the service provider. The service consumer queries the service registry to discover available services, and then sends requests to the service provider to invoke the service, processing the returned responses from the service provider. A typical example of a service consumer is an ecommerce website that uses a payment gateway API (see *service interface* below) to process customer payments.

- **Service registry**: Acts as a directory or repository where service providers register their services. Service consumers query the registry to discover and locate the services they need. The service registry stores metadata about services (e.g. service description, endpoint, supported operations, security policies) and facilitates service discovery by enabling service consumers to locate the appropriate service providers. A common implementation of a service registry is a universal description, discovery and integration (UDDI) registry or a modern API gateway.

- **Messaging/communication layer**: Provides the infrastructure for communication between the service consumer and provider, ensuring messages are transmitted securely and reliably. This element of the design facilitates message exchange using protocols such as HyperText Transfer Protocol (HTTP), SOAP, REST or Google Remote Procedure Call (gRPC) by handling the routing, transformation and security of messages (service requests). A common implementation of this is an enterprise service bus (ESB), or some other API management platform.

- **Service interface**: Defines how the service is accessed by specifying the inputs, outputs and communication protocols. The service interface acts as the contract between the service consumer and the service provider, ensuring consistent interaction regardless of the underlying implementation. A common implementation of a service interface is a Web Services Description Language (WSDL) file.

Figure 2.4 provides a straightforward overview of the key components of a SOD and how they are interconnected.

Figure 2.4 Overview of service-oriented design elements

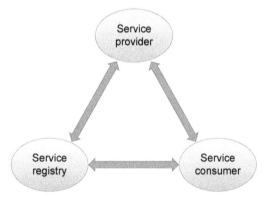

SOD and CBD share similar objectives but differ in scope and implementation. While CBD focuses on dividing a digital solution into small, reusable and replaceable software components, SOD breaks down the solution into independent, platform-agnostic, interoperable and loosely coupled services. Services tend to be more coarsely grained while components are more finely grained. Components usually communicate via method calls, function calls or direct access to interfaces, depending on the technology and architecture, which can result in tight coupling, whereas services are designed to be loosely coupled, with each being self-contained and having minimal dependencies on others. Communication between services is achieved through standard, platform-agnostic protocols such as SOAP or REST, commonly implemented as web services.

SOD is based around the following key principles:

- **Loose coupling**: Services are relatively independent of each other (meaning that changes to a component that implements a service do not inadvertently impact the service consumer), enabling flexibility in integration.

- **Reusability**: Services are designed to be reusable across multiple applications or contexts, reducing duplication of effort.

- **Standardised interfaces**: Communication between services occurs via well-defined, standard protocols, such as HTTP, SOAP, REST or gRPC.

- **Interoperability**: Services can be used by different digital solutions, regardless of their underlying technologies or platforms.

- **Encapsulation**: Services hide their implementation details, exposing only the necessary functionality through interfaces.

- **Composability**: Services can be combined to create complex workflows or applications.

By adopting these principles, SOD realises the following benefits:

- **Scalability**: Individual services can be scaled independently to meet demand.

- **Flexibility**: Services can be added or replaced without impacting existing ones.

- **Improved maintainability**: Modular design simplifies debugging, updating and testing.

- **Technology agnosticism**: Services can be built using different programming languages or technologies.

- **Reuse of business logic**: Common functionality can be packaged as services and reused across different applications.

While there are significant benefits to adopting a service-oriented approach to the design of a digital solution, it should be acknowledged that the service-oriented approach does have its challenges:

- **Management complexity**: Managing multiple services, especially in large-scale systems, can be challenging.

- **Network overhead**: Communication between distributed services can introduce latency and require robust error handling.

- **Security concerns**: Ensuring secure communication and access control between services is critical but can be complex.

- **Service dependencies**: Dependencies between services can lead to cascading failures (where the failure of one service triggers a chain reaction, causing other interconnected services to fail and potentially leading to widespread system disruption) if not effectively managed.

SOD is prevalent in a range of industries and types of digital solution. For example:

- **Ecommerce platforms**: An ecommerce system could have separate services for user authentication, product catalogues, order management and payment processing.

- **Banking systems**: A bank may use individual services for customer management, transaction processing, loan applications and fraud detection.

- **Healthcare systems**: Services might include patient records, appointment scheduling, billing and lab results.

Microservices

Microservices are a particular style of SOA, inspired by the ideas in domain-driven design (see later in this chapter), in particular the **bounded context** concept, which is an approach to decoupling services. Decoupling is discussed further in Chapter 7.

Newman (2020) describes microservices as:

> independently deployable services modelled around a business domain ... From a technology viewpoint, microservices expose the business capabilities that they encapsulate via one or more network endpoints. Microservices communicate with each other via these networks – making them a form of distributed system. They also encapsulate data storage and retrieval, exposing data, via well-defined interfaces. So databases are hidden inside the service boundary.

According to Newman, key characteristics of microservices include:

- modelled around a business domain – each service is focused on a specific business capability;
- technology agnostic;
- independently deployable;
- encapsulated via one or more network endpoints;
- communicate with each other via networks;
- encapsulate data storage and retrieval – microservices own their own data;
- expose data via well-defined interfaces (databases are hidden inside the service boundary); and
- decompose an application into smaller services that run as separate processes.

SOA is often confused with microservices architecture, but there are key differences:

- SOA services are typically larger and may rely on an ESB for communication, while microservices are smaller, more finely grained and often communicate using lightweight protocols such as REST.
- Microservices focus more on decentralised governance and deployment, whereas SOA often has more centralised control.

Microservices are considered further in Chapter 7.

DOMAIN-DRIVEN DESIGN

Domain-driven design (DDD) was introduced by Eric Evans (a software developer and consultant) in his book *Domain-Driven Design: Tackling Complexity in the Heart of Software* (Evans, 2004). The ideas behind DDD evolved over time as Evans worked on various software projects and encountered recurring problems related to understanding and modelling complex business domains. He observed that many software projects failed or faced significant challenges due to a lack of shared understanding between technical teams and domain experts, leading to a mismatch between the software model and the real-world problem it aimed to solve.

DDD is essentially a methodology aimed at bringing a deeper understanding of the business domain into the software development process. By providing a set of principles, patterns and practices, DDD helps developers to create software that better aligns with the real-world problems it seeks to address.

The main concept in DDD is that of a 'domain'. A 'domain' refers to the subject area or the problem space that the software system is being designed to address. It represents the knowledge, activities or concerns relating to a particular business area or application, and is composed of various interconnected concepts, rules and processes that are relevant to the problem at hand.

Emphasis is placed on understanding and modelling the domain to create a shared understanding between domain experts (usually business stakeholders) and software developers. By closely aligning the software model with the domain model, developers can create more effective and maintainable solutions that directly address the business problems at hand.

The modelling of the domain is an iterative process, which often involves ongoing communication and collaboration between domain experts and development teams to refine and evolve the understanding of the domain throughout the software development life cycle (SDLC).

There are a number of supporting concepts within DDD:

- **Bounded contexts**: Define explicit boundaries within which a particular model or terminology applies. Different parts of an organisation or system may have different bounded contexts with distinct models, which helps to manage complexity. A bounded context defines the scope within which a model is implemented, ensuring that each bounded context has its own distinct set of software artefacts.

- **Ubiquitous language**: DDD emphasises the importance of establishing a common language between technical and non-technical stakeholders. This shared vocabulary helps to bridge a common communication gap and ensures that everyone involved in the project has a clear and consistent understanding of the domain.

- **Entities, value objects and aggregates**: Specific modelling concepts are used, such as entities (objects with distinct identities), value objects (objects without distinct identities) and aggregates (clusters of entities and value objects). These concepts help to structure the domain model.

- **Agile development practices**: DDD embraces Agile development practices, including iterative development, continuous feedback and collaboration between developers and domain experts.

- **Strategic design and tactical design**: DDD distinguishes between strategic design, which focuses on the overall structure of the software system, and tactical design, which involves the detailed design decisions within a specific bounded context. According to Vernon (2016):

  > Strategic design is used like broad brushstrokes prior to getting into the details of implementation ... tactical design is like using a thin brush to paint the fine details of your domain model.

- **Context mapping**: Techniques such as 'context mapping' help to manage the interactions between different bounded contexts and ensure consistency in the overall system.

Figure 2.5 shows a context map for the learning and development domain within an HR department. It contains two bounded contexts (`Course Context` and `Exam Context`), represented by the ellipses, and a context mapping between them, represented by the curved line. The boxes in each bounded context represent entities of relevance to each context. `Booking` and `Learner` are entities common to both contexts and, hence, the need for a context mapping between the two bounded contexts.

Figure 2.5 Example context map

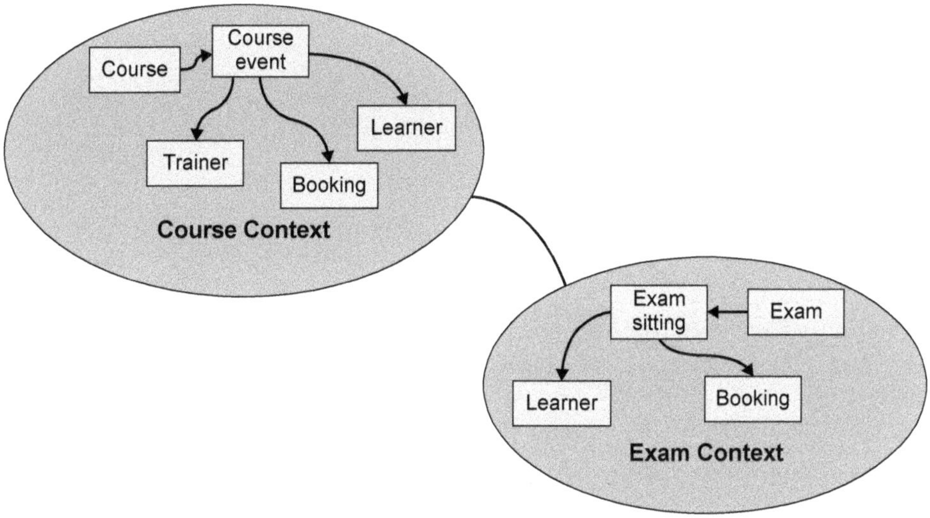

DDD has been widely adopted in various domains, particularly in projects dealing with complex business logic and intricate domain models. Although it was first introduced over 20 years ago, it has influenced current software development practices such as microservices, and remains relevant today as a valuable approach to building software systems that are both technically sound and aligned with the needs of the business.

LOGICAL AND PHYSICAL DESIGN

In addition to the particular approach or methodology to follow, another consideration facing designers of digital solutions is whether to produce an abstract version of their design (logical design) before specifying the implementation specifics of the solution (physical design).

The concepts of logical and physical design with regard to software and database systems have evolved over time as a result of the growing complexity of digital solutions, and the need for more structured and systematic approaches to design.

Logical design

As computing systems have become more sophisticated, designers recognised the importance of creating an abstract representation of the system's structure and functionality before diving into implementation details.

Logical design focuses on the logical organisation of system elements (data, processes, inputs and outputs) and their interrelationships, and aims to create a high-level, technology-independent (often referred to as platform-independent) blueprint that captures the essential structure and functionality of the system. For example, in the context of the design of databases, logical design involves defining the required structure of the data, including tables, relationships and constraints, irrespective of the technology that will be used to store and manipulate the data.

In software engineering, logical design pertains to the high-level representation of software architecture, functionality and other abstract representations that guide the development process.

Physical design

Early information systems were often closely tied to specific hardware and lacked the flexibility needed for evolving technologies. The need for a clear distinction between the logical representation of a system and its physical implementation emerged as systems became more complex and diverse.

Physical design involves translating a logical design into a platform-specific implementation, considering the use of specific hardware, software and communication technologies. It defines how data is stored, processed and communicated, incorporating decisions on infrastructure, networking, security and performance optimisation. This includes selecting appropriate database management systems (DBMSs), indexing strategies, partitioning, storage optimisation and system configurations to enhance efficiency. Additionally, it covers software implementation choices such as programming languages, algorithms and integration protocols to ensure seamless operation and scalability.

Ultimately, physical design ensures that a digital solution is optimised for real-world deployment, balancing performance, reliability and maintainability.

Rationale for separating logical and physical design

Although some designers may not produce a separate logical design, jumping straight to environment-specific implementation specifications, a common approach is to start with a platform-independent solution design (logical design) that is then 'tuned' to take advantage of the specifics of a particular technological implementation environment (physical design). This way a generic solution can be proposed and subsequently adapted for implementation in a range of different environments, using different technologies, which allows for greater flexibility and adaptability to changes in technology. This is how the design objective of portability is achieved.

The concepts of logical and physical design have evolved alongside the growth of computing and information systems, reflecting the need for systematic methods to handle the increasing complexity of technology and software development.

As technology is continuously evolving and new technologies are being introduced all the time, this book focuses predominantly on logical design. However, references to specific technologies are included where this helps to explain concepts and techniques that are specific to certain technologies.

DESIGN PATTERNS

Designers are often faced with similar challenges to those that have already been solved in the past. Rather than reinventing the wheel, so to speak, they go back to a previous design that was used to address a similar challenge, and use that as a template (pattern) for their current design. This approach has continued in an informal way for many years, but became more formalised with the advent of the seminal book *Design Patterns: Elements of Reusable Object-Oriented Software*, by Erich Gamma and others (Gamma et al., 1994).

Design patterns make it easier to reuse successful designs and architectures. In general, formally defined patterns have four essential elements:

- **Pattern name**: A memorable name that identifies the design problem that the pattern addresses.
- **Problem**: Describes when to apply the pattern by explaining the problem and its context.
- **Solution**: Describes the elements that make up the design, their relationships, responsibilities and collaborations. The solution is a template, an abstract description of how a general arrangement of elements can be used to solve the problem.
- **Consequences**: The results and trade-offs of applying the pattern, which help the designer to understand the benefits and disadvantages of doing so.

Gang of Four design patterns

Design Patterns: Elements of Reusable Object-Oriented Software (Gamma et al., 1994) introduced a set of template solutions to address a set of common design problems.

Each pattern is named, leading to the adoption of a common vocabulary for designers, who can simply refer to the names of design patterns rather than having to explain them to their peers. This has also led to a more standardised approach to software design across the IT industry.

The patterns presented by Gamma et al. (referred to as the Gang of Four design patterns) are independent of programming language, and so can be adopted during logical design and tuned during physical design. Most of the patterns are concerned with minimising coupling and maximising cohesion, explored further in Chapter 4. They achieve this through abstraction, composition and delegation, basic principles of object-oriented software development, which are also explored in *Delivering Digital Solutions*.

The Gang of Four design patterns are grouped into three categories: **creational patterns**, **structural patterns** and **behavioural patterns**. Table 2.1 provides a summary of the patterns. A detailed explanation of each pattern is beyond the scope of this book.

Table 2.1 Common design patterns (after Gamma et al., 1994)

Category	Pattern name	Description
Creational	Abstract factory	Provide an interface for creating families of related or dependent objects without specifying their concrete classes.
	Builder	Separate the construction of a complex object from its representation, allowing the same construction process to create various representations.
	Factory method	Define an interface for creating a single object, but let subclasses decide which class to instantiate.
	Virtual proxy/lazy initialisation	Delay the creation of an object, the calculation of a value or some other expensive process until the first time it is needed.
	Prototype	Specify the kinds of objects to create using a prototypical instance, and create new objects by copying this prototype.
	Singleton	Ensure a class has only one instance, and provide a global point of access to it.
Structural	Adapter (wrapper or translator)	Convert the interface of a class into another interface clients expect. An adapter that lets classes work together that could not otherwise because of incompatible interfaces.
	Bridge	Decouple an abstraction from its implementation, allowing the two to vary independently.
	Composite	Compose objects into tree structures to represent part–whole hierarchies. Composite lets clients treat individual objects and compositions of objects uniformly.

(Continued)

Table 2.1 (Continued)

Category	Pattern name	Description
	Decorator	Attach additional responsibilities to an object dynamically, keeping the same interface.
	Facade	Provide a unified interface to a set of interfaces in a subsystem. Facade defines a higher-level interface that makes the subsystem easier to use.
	Flyweight	Use sharing to support large numbers of similar objects efficiently.
	Proxy	Provide a surrogate or placeholder for another object to control access to it.
Behavioural	Chain of responsibility	Avoid coupling the sender of a request to its receiver by giving more than one object a chance to handle the request. Chain the receiving objects and pass the request along the chain until an object handles it.
	Command	Encapsulate a request as an object, thereby enabling the developer to parameterise clients with different requests, queue or log requests, and support undoable operations.
	Interpreter	Given a language, define a representation for its grammar along with an interpreter that uses the representation to interpret sentences in the language.
	Iterator	Provide a way to access the elements of an aggregate object sequentially without exposing its underlying representation.
	Mediator	Define an object that encapsulates how a set of objects interact. Mediator promotes loose coupling by keeping objects from referring to each other explicitly, and it enables the developer to vary their interaction independently.
	Memento	Without violating encapsulation, capture and externalise an object's internal state, enabling the object to be restored to this state later.
	Observer (publish/subscribe)	Define a one-to-many dependency between objects, where a state change in one object results in all its dependents being notified and updated automatically.
	State	Enable an object to alter its behaviour when its internal state changes.
	Strategy	Define a family of algorithms, encapsulate each one and make them interchangeable. Strategy enables the algorithm to vary independently from clients that use it.

(Continued)

Table 2.1 (Continued)

Category	Pattern name	Description
	Template method	Define the skeleton of an algorithm in an operation, deferring some steps to subclasses. The template method enables subclasses to redefine certain steps of an algorithm without changing the algorithm's structure.
	Visitor	Represent an operation to be performed on the elements of an object structure. Visitor enables the developer to define a new operation without changing the classes of the elements on which it operates.

Gamma et al. acknowledge that their book only captures a fraction of what an expert might know. It does not have any patterns dealing with concurrency, distributed programming or real-time programming. It does not include any application domain-specific patterns. However, since the publication of the book, the concept of patterns has been extended to other IT disciplines and now software architecture patterns, such as the model–view–controller pattern and analysis patterns are commonplace.

3 INPUT, OUTPUT AND USER INTERFACE DESIGN

INTRODUCTION

Input, output and user interface (UI) design is constantly evolving as new technologies become available for digital solutions. Given its broad scope, this field of design spans various disciplines and often necessitates collaboration with specialists with different areas of expertise. It is beyond the scope of this book to provide comprehensive coverage of all the skills, tools and technologies involved in the design of inputs, outputs and UIs, but there are some foundational concepts and principles that are relatively constant and that underpin this aspect of design. These provide the focus for this chapter.

As with all aspects of design, it all starts with requirements ...

IDENTIFYING INPUTS AND OUTPUTS FROM REQUIREMENTS

Input and output requirements are defined during Requirements Engineering and are typically specified in a solution backlog, requirements catalogue or functional specification. Therefore, a good start point for I/O design is the functional requirements from these artefacts.

A best practice within Requirements Engineering is to produce a model of the functional requirements (a functional model). A de facto standard notation used by business and system analysts for functional models is the UML **use case diagram**. Use case diagrams were introduced in Book 1 in this series.

Figure 3.1 shows an example use case diagram for a sales order processing solution. The inputs and outputs to be designed are clearly identified from the points where associations between actors and use cases cross the system boundary:

- order details;
- picking details;
- despatch details;
- delivery details;
- invoice details.

It is not possible from the diagram alone to determine whether each of the associations is an input, an output or a two-way dialogue. This is because the diagram on its own provides an incomplete definition of the functional requirements. The additional information required by the designer is contained in a set of **use case descriptions** that support the diagram and provide further elaboration of how the interactions will be played out between the actors (the customer, the picker, the logistics team, the driver and the accounts department shown in Figure 3.1) and the required system (identified by the named system boundary, in this case an order processing system) to achieve the goal, or desired outcome of the function in question.

Figure 3.1 Use case diagram for a sales order processing system

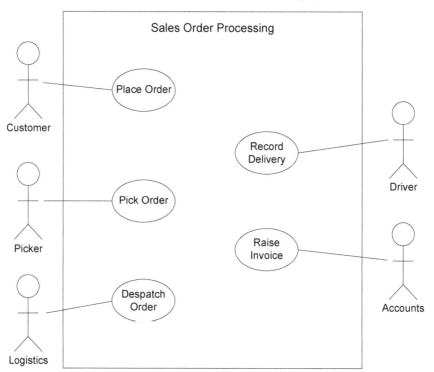

Use case descriptions, backlog items or requirements catalogue entries are often supplemented by prototypes of example screens, documents and reports, produced by the business or system analyst. These are developed to help further elaborate the functional requirements and bring to life the use case descriptions. Early prototypes may take the form of a sketch or storyboard, such as the example in Figure 3.2, which shows a series of screen sketches for the Place Order function of a smartphone app, along with navigation options between the screens.

Once the inputs and outputs have been identified, I/O design can proceed at two levels of granularity: macro design and micro design. At the macro level, the designer considers

Figure 3.2 A storyboard showing a series of screens for a smartphone app

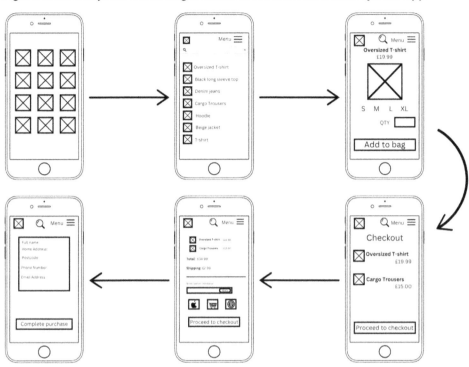

the overall mechanism for achieving the inputs and outputs, including the use of appropriate technologies. At the micro level, the designer focuses on the detailed design of the user interface, including content and layout of forms, reports and message file formats (in the case of interfaces with external systems).

SELECTION OF I/O TECHNOLOGIES

Quite often, the technologies to be used for inputs and outputs will have been predetermined when considering technical requirements during the definition of terms of reference for the project, or the subsequent Requirements Engineering work. For example, the project objective may be to develop a new website or a mobile app, and one of the technical requirements might impose a technical constraint to use a particular technology, such as 'the new app shall be compatible with iOS and Android mobile operating systems'.

Where the designer is breaking new ground, they may consider a range of potential technologies and select the most appropriate for the purpose. Where this is the case, they must pay particular attention to the nature of the application, the end-user and the environment within which the solution will be used. For example:

- The context of use may demand output devices that have certain security features, are tolerant to dirt and dust or which are mobile and can be handheld.

- An application to be used by staff in a restaurant to take payments and print receipts needs to be portable (handheld) and use a touch screen rather than a keyboard to minimise the size and weight of the device. It should also include an integral printer that uses thermal paper rather than ink or toner, which are too bulky.

- An application that needs to support a blind user may require the use of voice recognition as an input technology and potentially braille displays or text to voice as an output technology.

- The production of payslips for a payroll bureau will impose quality, volumetric and timing constraints necessitating the deployment of fast, high-quality printer technology.

- A self-service point-of-sale device in a grocery store may need touch screen displays that enable the user to browse items and select the required item by touching a picture on the screen.

- The scoreboard at a major sporting stadium will require large-scale electronic billboard technology to enable spectators to read from a significant distance.

While there are some technologies that support both inputs and outputs, such as a smartphone with a touch screen, it can be helpful to consider the two sets of technology separately.

Input technology

The principal objective of input design is:

> To determine and specify how the solution will collect data in its raw form (e.g. a paper-based document or a third-party digital solution) and convert that data into an internal format that the system can understand.[1]

To understand the decisions that the designer makes during input design, and, in particular, during the selection of appropriate input technology, it is first necessary to understand how the input process works. Figure 3.3, which has been reproduced with permission from Assist Knowledge Development Ltd, shows the various stages involved.

Original recording   Data is created or captured at its source. Historically this was achieved using a handwritten data capture form, although modern digital solutions capture data using a number of different mechanisms, as explored later in this chapter.

---

1   All computers use a binary code internally, which uses only the two binary digits 0 and 1.

Figure 3.3 Stages during data input (© Assist Knowledge Development Ltd)

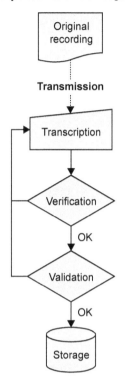

Transmission	The captured data is transferred to some location where it is converted into an internal format understandable by the system (transcription). Today, digital solutions tend to achieve the transmission electronically and sometimes the transcription process is performed within the same device as the data capture, thus not requiring transmission, other than some internal data transfer within the device.
Transcription	The captured data is converted (transcribed) into a computer-readable format. Historically this would have been achieved by a data entry operator 'keying' the data using a keyboard, but, again, modern digital solutions have a number of options available, discussed later.
Verification and validation	Verification and validation are often performed together, but logically verification should be performed first. While the data transcription process is being performed, the transcribed data is checked to ensure that no errors are introduced (verification). Common errors are a data entry operator mis-keying some data or a scanner misreading a barcode or text. Such errors are referred to as **transcription errors**.

Once verified, the transcribed data is considered a 'true'[2] representation of the source data. It is then subjected to further checks to ensure that it complies with predefined data integrity principles and business rules (validation).

Storage   The final stage is to store the data in a permanent or semi-permanent storage system for future use. This is sometimes referred to as persistent data storage.

The designer needs to make decisions covering the above stages to ensure that the approach taken meets the overall objective identified above, but also takes account of the following sub-objectives:

- **Minimise the amount of data recorded**: The more data to be captured, the greater the effort, cost and time required to collect, transmit and transcribe the data, and the higher the likelihood of error.

- **Minimise data transmission**: Each transmission of data incurs cost, has the potential to delay the input process and increases the chance of errors being introduced.

- **Minimise data transcription**: Transcribing data from one form into another increases the chance of error and incurs cost and delay.

- **Verify and validate to ensure accuracy**: Choose appropriate checks based upon the nature of the data involved and the data capture environment. Verification and validation are types of system control and are discussed further in Chapter 6.

- **Choose appropriate input technologies**: The chosen technology should support the needs of the intended user while being appropriate to the context of use – the application (timing requirements, data volumes and so on) and target data capture environment.

While the above considerations will influence the choice of technology to be used, the designer must also consider the following:

- **Efficiency**: The chosen input mechanism should make efficient use of resources, such as processor time, memory and mains power.

- **Availability**: The system must be available whenever it is needed, without fail.

- **Resilience**: Exceptional situations and errors must be handled in a controlled manner.

- **Timing**: Any delay during the data collection and transcription process must be minimised.

- **Accuracy**: The potential to introduce errors in the final stored data must be minimised.

---

2   Verification is derived from 'veritas', meaning truth.

- **Usability**: The approach taken should be easy for the user to perform and support their level of ability (see also *User interface design* below).

- **Accessibility**: (1) Input elements should be accessible to users with disabilities by following accessibility standards;[3] (2) alternative input methods should be used for users with different needs; (3) input methods should work seamlessly across different devices and screen sizes; (4) touch screen-friendly designs should be considered for mobile devices.

- **Data security and privacy**: Appropriate mechanisms should be implemented to protect sensitive user information in order to comply with data protection legislation and prevent unauthorised users from accessing or modifying data.

- **Internationalisation and localisation**: Different languages, date formats and cultural norms should be accommodated. Ensure that input validation considers regional variations.

- **Scalability**: It is likely that there will be an increase in the volume of inputs over time so the input mechanism must be designed to scale with the growth of data and user interactions.

- **Compliance**: The design must comply with relevant laws and regulations and adhere to industry-specific standards and best practices.

- **Cost**: The cost of using a particular approach/technology/mechanism must not outweigh the benefits derived from using it.

A further consideration during input design is whether the input must be undertaken in real time (often referred to as 'online') or whether it can be batched and processed at a later time (e.g. overnight). Key factors in deciding whether a batch input approach may be more practical are the volumes of data being captured/processed, the timing constraints of the application and the costs involved. Online data input is more desirable from a business perspective, but it is sometimes difficult to justify the costs involved, and so batch processes become a more practical solution.

Designers must be familiar with a wide range of technologies so that they can select those most appropriate to support the solution requirements. Different technologies score differently in terms of the considerations identified above.

Input devices can be classified as direct or indirect. Indirect input devices require a human user to interpret the source data and translate it into key presses or some other form of interaction with the system. Direct input devices enable capture and transcription into a computer-readable format without the need for a human user to undertake any translation, thus significantly reducing transcription errors.

Table 3.1 provides a list of the most common input technologies, with typical uses. A detailed explanation of these technologies is outside the scope of this book.

---

3 Web Content Accessibility Guidelines (WCAG) published by the World Wide Web Consortium (W3C) is the de facto standard for modern digital solutions.

Table 3.1 Popular input technologies

Technology/device	Uses
Keyboard	Traditional input device for typing text and executing commands.
Touch screen	Allows users to interact with a display by touching it directly. Commonly used in smartphones, tablets and interactive kiosks. Can be useful for novice users (such as patients arriving at doctors' surgeries) or applications that require high-volume, rapid data entry (such as point-of-sale terminals in retail outlets). Portable devices are used extensively in logistics applications to record status updates for orders at various stages throughout the fulfilment cycle and when combined with a stylus, can capture signatures to provide evidence of successful completion of a transaction (such as a delivery).
Mouse	Pointing device used for navigating graphical user interfaces (GUIs) and interacting with on-screen elements. Although rapidly being replaced by touch screens, a mouse can be used as an alternative or addition to keyboard entry, to simplify the selection of information, to resize pictures, drag and drop and so on.
Trackpad/touchpad	A touch-sensitive surface on laptops or external devices that allows users to control the cursor by swiping, tapping or other gestures (see *gesture recognition* below).
Stylus	A digital pen used for drawing, writing or interacting with touch-sensitive devices, such as smartphones, tablets or touch screen laptops.
Voice recognition	Enables users to control devices or input text using spoken commands. Often used to automate high-volume data entry (thus reducing costs and minimising delays) or for hands-free use, or for accessibility for users with physical disabilities.
Gesture recognition	Uses physical movements or gestures to control and interact with touchpad or touch screen devices. Often found in motion-sensing technologies and smartphone gesture controls.
Bar code scanner	Used to input data by scanning a pre-printed code (in the form of a series of vertical bars of different widths). Commonly used in retail to encode product information for fast, high-volume scanning at point of sale terminals. Also extensively used in logistics and inventory management. Use of newer quick response (QR) codes provides rapid access to a wealth of information by extending accessibility to individuals with an appropriate app on their smartphone.
Document scanner	In addition to scanning bar codes and QR codes, scanners can be used to scan documents to produce a digitised image or to convert the contents to text or some other form of coded data (see also *Optical character recognition* and *Optical mark recognition* below).

(Continued)

Table 3.1 (Continued)

Technology/device	Uses
Optical character recognition (OCR)	Used with document scanners to recognise characters and words and convert them into a format that can be read by word processing and similar applications. Particularly suited to large-volume document processing where the range of possible inputs is varied, such as handwritten and printed forms and questionnaires.
Optical mark recognition (OMR)	Similar to OCR, but where the range of possible inputs is limited to basic marks drawn on a pre-printed form, such as UK lottery tickets or multiple-choice examination answer sheets.
Magnetic ink character recognition (MICR)	Similar to OCR but only recognises characters printed in special magnetic ink. Used mainly in the banking industry for processing cheques and transaction vouchers, to counteract fraud.
Radio frequency identification (RFID)	A transponder device reads the data encoded on an RFID chip as the chip passes it. Used for high-volume transactions where the amount of data to be captured is limited (e.g. just a unique identifier). Data capture can be both active (e.g. a user swiping an Oyster card over a reader in a London Underground station) or passive (e.g. an engine passing a sensor on a car assembly line).
Smart card	Cards embedded with chips that can be used for authentication or data storage. See also *Radio frequency identification* above.
Biometric input	Includes fingerprint scanners, facial recognition and other biometric technologies for secure authentication.
Camera input	Utilises cameras for capturing images, recognising objects or interpreting gestures. Often used with artificial intelligence (AI) systems such as virtual reality (VR), augmented reality (AR) and smart devices such as driverless vehicles.
Game controller/ joystick	Input devices designed for gaming, including joysticks, gamepads and steering wheels.
Specialist controller	Used for specialised applications such as flight simulators or control systems.
Brain–computer interface (BCI)	Interfaces that translate brain signals into commands for digital systems. This is a niche technology with limited practical uses, but could become beneficial to enhance accessibility for users with certain physical disabilities.

Output technology

The principal objective of output design is:

To define how data that is stored and/or manipulated by a digital solution will be extracted and presented, in a format that can be interpreted and used to meet relevant functional requirements defined during Requirements Engineering.

The recipient of outputs is either the end-user of the solution or another digital solution.

In addition to ensuring that the functional requirements are met, the designer must also take account of a number of other considerations (many of which are also common to input design, described above):

- **Efficiency**: The output should make efficient use of resources, such as processor time, memory, mains power, and consumables such as paper and toner/ink.

- **Timing/response times**: Appropriate technology should be selected to optimise loading and processing times to minimise delay in generating outputs.

- **Resilience**: The chosen technology should be robust enough to cope with predicted output volumes and work effectively in the target environment.

- **Accuracy**: Data output from the system should be correct and up to date.

- **Usability**: Outputs should be easy for the user to obtain and interpret.

- **Accessibility**: (1) Outputs should be accessible to users with disabilities by following accessibility standards such as WCAG; (2) alternative methods should be used for users with different needs; (3) outputs should work seamlessly across different devices and screen sizes.

- **Clarity**: The format and content of the output should be clearly understood by its intended recipient, ideally without separate instructions to clarify.

- **Relevance**: The output should provide only the data that is required to fulfil its purpose; any data beyond this will detract from its purpose and compromise its effectiveness. Excessive data may also contravene data protection legislation.

- **Quality**: The required quality of the output will often be determined by whether it is intended for personal or internal use, or for distribution to external stakeholders, such as customers. The intended audience may warrant higher-quality outputs, but where the outputs are for personal or internal use, it may not be necessary to produce such high-quality outputs. There may also be regulatory or legal requirements, or industry standards governing the precise specification of certain outputs.

- **Data security and privacy**: Appropriate mechanisms should be implemented to protect sensitive information and prevent unauthorised access to outputs and data, to comply with data protection legislation.

- **Internationalisation and localisation**: Different languages, date formats and cultural norms should be supported to accommodate regional variations.

- **Scalability**: The design should consider the potential increase in the volume of outputs over time, and an appropriate technology selected that can handle potential future volumes.

- **Compliance**: *As input design.*

- **Cost**: *As input design.*

As with input design, one of the key decisions that the designer must make is the choice of technology to use, taking account of the above considerations. Table 3.2 provides a summary of the most popular output technologies and their potential uses.

Table 3.2 Popular output technologies

Technology/device	Uses
Monitor	Suitable for most output requirements. However, depending on the size and quality requirements, there are a number of different technologies available. Some of the more common technologies include: • **Liquid crystal display (LCD) monitors**: Thin, lightweight, energy-efficient and available in various sizes. • **Light emitting diode (LED) monitors**: Energy-efficient, better contrast ratios and slimmer profiles compared to traditional LCDs. • **Organic light emitting diode (OLED) monitors**: Offer vibrant colours, high contrast ratios, faster response times and true blacks. • **Curved monitors**: Enhanced viewing angles, reduced glare and a more natural field of view for certain applications. • **High refresh rate monitors**: Smoother motion, reduced motion blur and improved gaming experiences. • **High dynamic range (HDR) monitors**: Improved contrast, richer colours and a more lifelike visual experience. • **Ultra-high definition (UHD) monitors**: 4K offers four times the resolution of full HD;[4] 8K offers eight times the resolution of full HD, providing sharper and more detailed images. *Note: these technologies are not mutually exclusive. For example, it is possible to have an 8K OLED, UHD, HDR monitor.*
Touch screen	Similar to monitors but have the additional benefit of doubling up as an input device. Commonly used in laptops, smartphones and tablet devices, but specialist devices are also common in retail and logistics applications.
Digital/data projectors	Display digital content on fixed or portable large screens or surfaces. Commonly used to display visual content for meetings, lectures, training courses and conferences.
LED/LCD walls	Large-scale displays used in public spaces for advertising, information display or artistic installations.

(Continued)

---

4 'Full HD' (also referred to as 1080p) refers to a display resolution of 1920 × 1080 pixels, commonly used in monitors and television screens.

Table 3.2 (Continued)

Technology/device	Uses
Printer	Printers are used for permanent hard copies of output. Different printer technologies are suited to different uses. For example: • **Laser printers**: Good for high-volume printing as they have a high pages per minute (PPM) rate. • **Inkjet printers**: Lower cost than lasers and are generally used where cost-effective colour output is required. Some inkjets produce high-quality photographs and are referred to as photo printers. • **Thermal printers**: Used for mobile applications (e.g. hand-held credit card machines) and high-volume, small-format outputs (e.g. till receipts). • **Impact printers** (e.g. dot-matrix and drum printers): All but extinct now, having been superseded by laser and inkjet printers. However, some are still used where multi-part, carbon copy stationery is used with legacy applications. • **3D printers**: Create physical objects layer by layer from digital models. Used in manufacturing for rapid prototyping of new products, in healthcare for 3D-printed prosthetics and orthotics and patient-specific implants, and many other industries (e.g. aerospace, automotive, construction, architecture, fashion and jewellery, arts and entertainment, consumer goods and customisation, defence and security).
Plotter	Specialised output devices designed for producing large-format prints and drawings with precise and accurate details. They are commonly used with computer-aided design (CAD) applications in engineering, architecture, cartography and other fields that require high-quality, large-scale graphical output.
F-ink/electronic paper displays	Mimic the appearance of ink on paper, often used in ebook readers.
Braille displays	Converts digital text into Braille for visually impaired users.
Speakers, earphones and headphones	Provides sound output for system alerts and applications such as gaming, multimedia and specialist audio processing, or where text-to-speech (TTS) technology is used, such as to read back inputs made using voice recognition technology or screen readers used to realise accessibility requirements for visually impaired users. Headsets combine speakers with a microphone to act as both an input and output device.
Haptic feedback devices	Vibration motors used in smartphones, game controllers and wearables to provide tactile feedback.

(Continued)

Table 3.2 (Continued)

Technology/device	Uses
AR/VR glasses	Display digital information in the user's field of view. Used with AR/VR applications.
Digital signage	Used for information dissemination and wayfinding in public spaces.
Digital scoreboards	Used to display scores, statistics and other relevant information during sporting and other events.
Electronic billboard	Similar to digital signage. Used for advertising and public announcements.
Notification systems (LED lights, alerts, pop-ups)	Used to inform users about system events or messages.
LED indicators	Status lights to provide visual feedback about device or system status.
Head-up display (HUD)	Projects information onto a transparent screen in the user's field of view. Used primarily for in-car displays and aviation.
Text to speech (TTS)	A type of speech synthesis that enables a computer or other digital device to read aloud text-based content. TTS is integrated into assistive technology devices such as screen readers that make written information accessible to individuals who have difficulty reading, such as those with visual impairments or learning disabilities. Other common uses of TTS include: • **Navigation**: TTS enables Global Positioning System (GPS) navigation systems to provide spoken directions to drivers, pedestrians or cyclists. • **E-learning and educational tools**: TTS enables educational software, e-learning platforms and digital textbooks to read educational content aloud, aiding students in comprehension. • **Voice assistants**: Virtual assistants such as Apple's Siri, Google Assistant and Amazon's Alexa use TTS to respond to user queries and provide information in spoken form. • **Communication devices**: TTS enables individuals with speech impairments to communicate through synthesised speech technology integrated into augmentative and alternative communication (AAC) devices. • **Ebook readers and word processors**: Provide 'read-aloud' features to enable users to listen to the text instead of reading it.
Short Message Service (SMS) and Multimedia Messaging Service (MMS)	Used with mobile devices (typically smartphones, smartwatches and tablets) to provide an immediate alert direct to the end-user, wherever they are located.

(Continued)

Table 3.2 (Continued)

Technology/device	Uses
Email	Similar to SMS and MMS but also used for confirmatory messages that are typically less critical, or to send documents as attachments.
Digital media (magnetic, solid-state, optical)	Data is output to digital media for storage or transportation purposes. There are a number of different technologies employed: • magnetic media (magnetic tape, magnetic disk); • solid-state media (SD cards, Universal Serial Bus (USB) memory sticks); • optical media (compact disc (CD),[5] digital video disc (DVD),[6] Blu-ray). Other than specialist applications in the film, television and music industries, digital media use tends to be limited to backup systems and archiving historical data to permanent 'hard-copy' for ad hoc reference.
eXtensible Markup Language (XML)	A widely used **markup language**[7] designed to store and transport data in a human- and machine-readable self-descriptive format. Primarily used for representing and transferring structured data, both internally (between components within an application) and externally (between disparate systems), due to it being an open standard. While XML itself is a standard, there are additional standards and specifications associated with XML to ensure consistency and interoperability, including generic standards (e.g. SOAP)[8] and industry- and application-specific standards, such as HR-XML for human resources (HR) systems, Financial products Markup Language (FpML) for financial products, Financial Information eXchange Markup Language (FIXML) for the exchange of financial information and ONline Information eXchange (ONIX) for publishing industry applications.

---

5 There are a number of variants of CD, including CD-Audio, CD-ROM, CD-R, CD-RW and CD-ROM/XA; coverage of these is beyond the scope of this book.

6 There are a number of variants of DVD, including DVD-Audio, DVD-Video, DVD-ROM, DVD-R, DVD+R, DVD-RW, DVD+RW and DVD-RAM; coverage of these is beyond the scope of this book.

7 A markup language is a mechanism for annotating a document in a way that is distinguishable from the document text itself. The annotations (or 'marks') are typically embedded in the text and provide information about the structure, presentation or meaning of the document.

8 SOAP is a protocol for exchanging structured information in web services, allowing programs running on different operating systems to communicate with each other.

USER INTERFACE DESIGN

Once the designer has identified the required inputs and outputs, and selected the most effective mechanism (including the technology to be used) to achieve them – referred to earlier as the macro-level design – they can turn their attention to the detailed mechanics of each input and output, in terms of the specific ways that the user will interact with the chosen I/O devices (micro-level I/O design or UI design).

User experience versus user interface

Before exploring UI design further, it is useful to distinguish between user interface and user experience (UX). ISO 9241-210:2019 (ISO, 2019) defines UX as:

> [A person's] perceptions and responses that result from the use and/or anticipated use of a system, product or service.

UX encompasses the overall experience and satisfaction a user has while interacting with a product or service. It includes the user's perceptions, emotions and responses to every aspect of the product, from initial awareness to usage and post-interaction reflections.

De Voil (2020) suggests there are five key elements to UX:

- a person;
- a system;
- use of, or interaction with, the system by the person;
- the perceptions of the person resulting from their use of the system; and
- the person's responses resulting from their use of the system.

UI, on the other hand, is a subset of UX that focuses on the visual elements, layouts and interactive components that users interact with when using a digital solution. The goal of UI design is to enhance the user's experience by optimising the way users interact with and navigate through a product. UI design therefore involves creating the visual presentation and ensuring the usability of the interface.

A well-designed UI contributes to a positive user experience, but a good user experience goes beyond the visual interface to encompass the overall journey and satisfaction of the user.

UI design principles

ISO 9241-210:2019 provides requirements and recommendations for human-centred design principles and activities and is particularly aimed at designers of computer-based interactive systems. UI design should ideally be based on the six principles of human-centred design (HCD), which is also known as user-centred design (UCD):

1. The design is based upon an explicit understanding of users, tasks and environments.

2. Users are involved throughout design and development.

3. The design is driven and refined by user-centred evaluation.

4. The process is iterative.

5. The design addresses the whole user experience.

6. The design team includes multidisciplinary skills and perspectives.

A key focus of UI design is to realise usability and accessibility non-functional requirements (NFR)s, defined during Requirements Engineering.

Usability

Jakob Nielsen (1994), a renowned usability expert, introduced a set of heuristics (guidelines) known as 'Nielsen's usability heuristics' (Table 3.3), which provide a set of broad principles intended to help evaluate the usability of UIs. Despite having been defined some 30 years ago, they are still widely used in UI design to identify potential issues and improve the overall usability of a system.

Table 3.3 Nielsen's usability heuristics

Heuristic	Implications for UI design
1. Visibility of system status	Users should be kept informed about what is happening within the system at all times. Provide feedback on the status of their interactions, such as progress indicators or loading animations.
2. Match between system and the real world	The system's language, concepts and actions should mirror the user's mental model and real-world expectations. Use familiar terminology and representations to minimise cognitive load.
3. User control and freedom	Users should have the ability to undo actions and easily navigate the system. Provide 'emergency exits' or clearly labelled options for users to recover from errors or unintended actions.
4. Consistency and standards	Follow established conventions and standards to create a consistent UI. Consistency helps users to predict the location and behaviour of interface elements.
5. Error prevention	Design the system to prevent errors wherever possible. This can include confirmation dialogues for irreversible actions or clear and straightforward form validation.

(Continued)

Table 3.3 (Continued)

Heuristic	Implications for UI design
6. Recognition rather than recall	Reduce the user's memory load by making information visible and easily retrievable. Avoid relying on user memory and provide cues and prompts to aid recognition.
7. Flexibility and efficiency of use	Design for both novice and expert users. Provide shortcuts, accelerators and efficient paths for experienced users while maintaining accessibility for beginners.
8. Aesthetic and minimalist design	Strive for a clean and minimalist design that avoids unnecessary information and distractions. An aesthetically pleasing design contributes to a positive user experience.
9. Help users recognise, diagnose and recover from errors	Clearly communicate error messages, providing constructive guidance on how to fix the issue. Help users to understand the problem and guide them towards a solution.
10. Help and documentation	Ideally, the system should be self-explanatory and intuitive. However, if assistance is required, provide easily accessible help documentation. Ensure that documentation is concise and task-focused.

Accessibility

Accessibility principles are guidelines and best practices designed to ensure that digital solutions are usable by people with diverse abilities and disabilities. Adhering to accessibility principles promotes inclusivity and ensures that everyone, regardless of their physical or cognitive abilities, can access and interact with digital content.

Table 3.4 lists the four accessibility principles defined by the W3C as part of their Web Accessibility Initiative (WAI). These principles are embodied in the W3C WCAG[9] standard, a de facto industry standard for accessibility. Table 3.4 includes some example guidance for each principle.

UI paradigms

The concept of design patterns was introduced in Chapter 2, and the Gang of Four patterns defined by Gamma et al. (1994) were introduced. However, while the principle of a design pattern can also apply to UI design, patterns in this context are typically referred to as UI paradigms.

Also known as interaction paradigms, UI paradigms are conceptual models that define the way users interact with and experience a user interface. They provide a framework for designing and organising the elements of a UI to enhance usability, accessibility and overall user satisfaction. Various UI paradigms have emerged over time, each with its

---

9   As at the time of writing (March 2025), the latest published version of WCAG is 2.2; a working draft of version 3.0 was published on 12 December 2024.

Table 3.4 Accessibility principles and guidelines

Principle	Example guidance
Perceivability	• Use legible font sizes and provide sufficient colour contrast between text and background to enhance readability.
	• Ensure that non-text content (such as images, videos and audio) has text alternatives, making it accessible to users who may not be able to perceive the non-text content.
	• Provide captions for multimedia content and transcriptions for audio content to support users with hearing impairments.
Operability	• Ensure that all functionality can be operated using a keyboard. Keyboard accessibility is crucial for users who may have difficulty using a mouse or other pointing device.
	• Allow users sufficient time to read and complete tasks. Avoid time limits that may be challenging for users with cognitive impairments.
Understandability	• Maintain a clear and consistent layout and predictable navigation structure to help users understand and navigate the content easily.
	• Provide clear error messages and suggest solutions to users when errors occur. Make sure users can easily identify and correct errors.
Robustness	• Ensure that digital content is accessible and usable across various devices and screen sizes.
	• Test and optimise content for compatibility with different web browsers to ensure a consistent experience for all users.
	• Employ semantic HyperText Markup Language (HTML) to convey the meaning and structure of content effectively. This helps assistive technologies to interpret and present the content accurately.
	• Ensure compatibility with various assistive technologies, such as screen readers, by testing content and interfaces with these tools.

own principles and characteristics. Table 3.5 provides a summary of the most common ones.

UI paradigms evolve over time, influenced by technological advancements, user preferences and design trends. Designers often choose or combine paradigms based on the specific requirements and context of the application or system they are working on.

Table 3.5 UI paradigms

Paradigm	Description
Command line interface (CLI)	Users interact with the system by typing text-based commands. Examples include Microsoft's Command Prompt and Apple's Terminal app.
Graphical user interface (GUI)	Users interact with the system through graphical elements such as icons, windows, buttons and menus. Typical examples include Windows, macOS and Linux desktop operating systems, and iOS and Android mobile operating systems.
Windows, Icons, Menus, Pointing Device (WIMP)	Extends the GUI paradigm with a focus on windows, icons, menus and pointing devices, such as a mouse or trackpad. Used extensively in desktop and mobile applications.
Web UI/ browser-based UI	Refers to websites and web applications designed to be accessed through web browsers, typically using HTML, cascading style sheets (CSSs) and JavaScript.
Touch user interface	Interfaces designed for touch-sensitive devices, such as smartphones and tablets. Typical examples include iOS, Android and Windows touch interfaces.
Voice user interface (VUI)	Users interact with the system using spoken language, often through voice-activated virtual assistants. Typical examples include Amazon's Alexa, Google Assistant and Apple's Siri.
Augmented reality (AR) UI	Interfaces that overlay digital information onto the real-world environment, enhancing the user's perception. Primarily used with AR headsets.
Virtual reality (VR) UI	Similar to AR UI, but for immersive virtual experiences rather than augmented applications, games and simulators. Primarily used with VR headsets.
Natural user interface (NUI)	Interfaces that leverage natural human actions and gestures for interaction. Typical examples include motion-sensing technologies, touch, voice and gesture controls.
Flat design	A design approach characterised by minimalistic elements, simple typography and a focus on clarity and usability. Typical examples include modern versions of iOS and Microsoft Design Language (formerly Windows Metro Design).
Material design	A design language developed by Google that emphasises a clean and consistent visual aesthetic inspired by material surfaces and textures. Typical examples include Android applications and Google web services.
Responsive design	A design approach that ensures a consistent user experience across different screen sizes and devices. Typical examples include websites that adapt to various screen resolutions.

UI design techniques

There are a range of techniques available to designers of digital solutions to help them create visually appealing, intuitive and user-friendly interfaces. Wireframes (see the example in Figure 3.4) and prototypes (technically a wireframe is a form of prototype) are arguably the most popular techniques, but other methods and approaches are in common use.

Figure 3.4 Example wireframe for an order capture screen

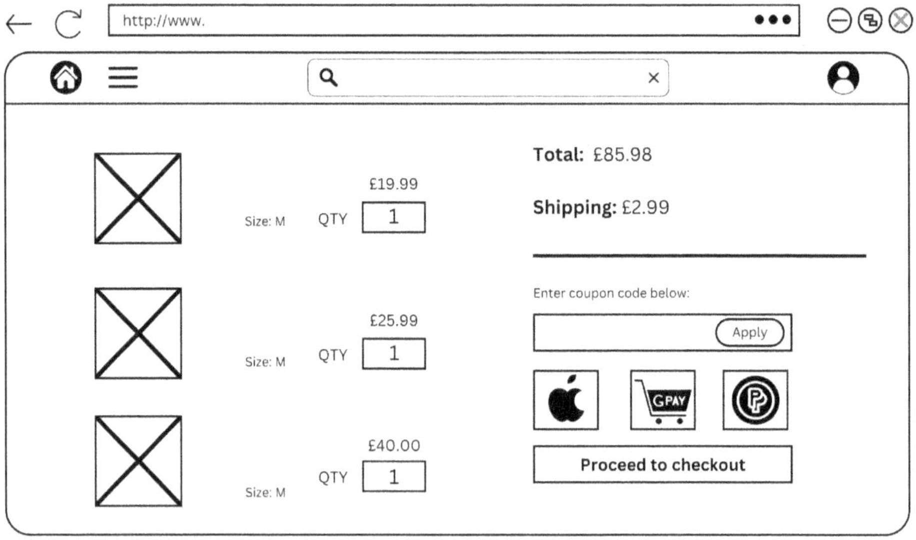

Table 3.6 summarises the most commonly used UI design techniques.

User analysis and personas

Key to designing good UIs and providing an excellent user experience is a detailed understanding of the potential users who will be interacting with the digital solution. This work will typically have been started by business analysts as part of Requirements Engineering, with the definition of user roles and personas, but can be supplemented by a specialist user researcher who may use user interviews, surveys, card sorting and usability testing (incorporating A/B testing) to understand the needs and preferences of the target audience and gain insights into user behaviours, expectations and pain points to inform design decisions.

Personas can help the designer to understand users' needs, experiences, behaviours and goals. Developed by Alan Cooper (Cooper et al., 2014), an American software designer and programmer who is widely recognised as the 'Father of Visual Basic', personas are fictional characters that embody the characteristics, behaviours, needs, limitations (in particular affecting accessibility and usability) and goals of a representative group of

Table 3.6 UI design techniques

Technique	Description
Wireframing	Low-fidelity sketches or wireframes outline the basic structure and layout of the UI without detailed design elements. This helps in early-stage conceptualisation and structuring of the interface. Wireframes typically exhibit zero functionality, although some tools have the ability to include links between wireframes to emulate the navigation through the UI.
Prototyping	High-fidelity, interactive prototypes simulate the UI's functionality and flow. This enables testing of interactions and workflows, gathering feedback and refining the design before implementation.
Style guides	Style guides define a set of design guidelines, including colour schemes, typography, iconography and other visual elements, to maintain consistency across the UI. They ensure a cohesive and uniform look and feel, simplifying the design process and enhancing user recognition.
Card sorting	A UX research method that helps the designer to understand how users categorise information and organise content by gaining insights into users' mental models, preferences and expectations regarding the organisation of information in order to inform design decisions for the structure of content and navigation throughout the interface.
A/B testing	Provides data-driven insights into design choices, helping to refine and optimise the user experience by comparing two versions (A and B) of an interface to determine which performs better based on user metrics.

users that might use a digital solution in a similar way. These detailed and semi-fictional profiles are based on real user data, research and insights, and serve as archetypes that help teams to understand and empathise with their target audience, providing a humanised perspective to help guide design decisions around how the solution will meet the needs of that particular persona, without describing an actual person.

Personas typically incorporate the following elements:

- **Demographics**: Details such as age, gender, occupation, education level and location. These demographic factors help in understanding the context of the persona's life.

- **Background and biography**: A brief narrative or backstory about the persona, including their professional background, interests and any relevant personal details. This helps to create a more humanised and relatable character.

- **Goals and objectives**: Describes what the persona aims to achieve by using a product or service. Understanding their goals helps to align design decisions with user needs.

- **Challenges and pain points**: Identifies the problems, obstacles or pain points that the persona may encounter in their interactions with the product or service. This guides the design team in addressing user concerns.

- **Behaviours and habits**: Explores the typical behaviours, habits and patterns of the persona, both in their daily life and in their use of digital products. This information informs user interactions and experiences.

- **Needs and expectations**: Outlines the persona's needs, expectations and preferences regarding the product or service. This helps to prioritise features and functionality.

- **Technology proficiency**: Assesses the persona's familiarity and comfort with technology. This is crucial for tailoring the user interface and experience accordingly.

- **User journey**: Maps out the journey the user follows from awareness to adoption and regular use of the product or service. This highlights key touchpoints and interactions.

Figure 3.5 shows a series of example personas for an online shopping solution.

User journey maps

Similar to customer journey maps, but narrower in scope, user journey maps focus on a user's experience with a particular product or service, typically a digital product such as a website or mobile app. The purpose of creating user journey maps is to understand how users interact with a specific product or service and identify areas for improvement in usability, user satisfaction and task completion rates. They can also be useful to inform the UI design for replacement or completely new products.

Figure 3.6 shows a typical user journey for purchasing groceries from an online store, based on the persona Robert from Figure 3.5.

Figure 3.5 Example personas

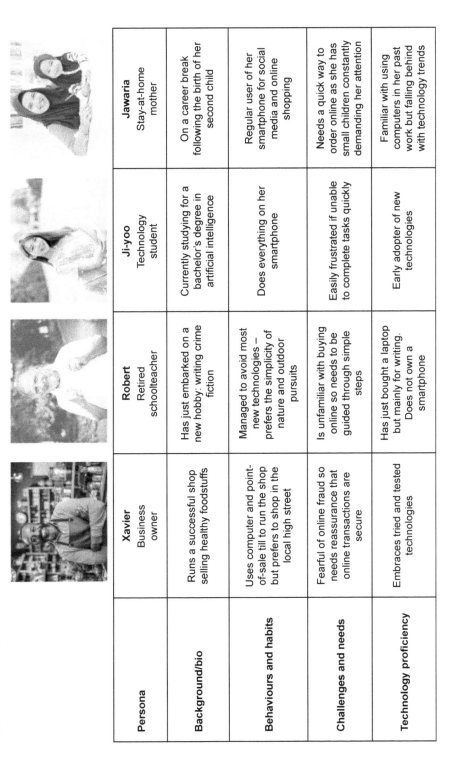

Persona	**Xavier** Business owner	**Robert** Retired schoolteacher	**Ji-yoo** Technology student	**Jawaria** Stay-at-home mother
Background/bio	Runs a successful shop selling healthy foodstuffs	Has just embarked on a new hobby: writing crime fiction	Currently studying for a bachelor's degree in artificial intelligence	On a career break following the birth of her second child
Behaviours and habits	Uses computer and point-of-sale till to run the shop but prefers to shop in the local high street	Managed to avoid most new technologies – prefers the simplicity of nature and outdoor pursuits	Does everything on her smartphone	Regular user of her smartphone for social media and online shopping
Challenges and needs	Fearful of online fraud so needs reassurance that online transactions are secure	Is unfamiliar with buying online so needs to be guided through simple steps	Easily frustrated if unable to complete tasks quickly	Needs a quick way to order online as she has small children constantly demanding her attention
Technology proficiency	Embraces tried and tested technologies	Has just bought a laptop but mainly for writing. Does not own a smartphone	Early adopter of new technologies	Familiar with using computers in her past work but falling behind with technology trends

51

Figure 3.6 Example user journey

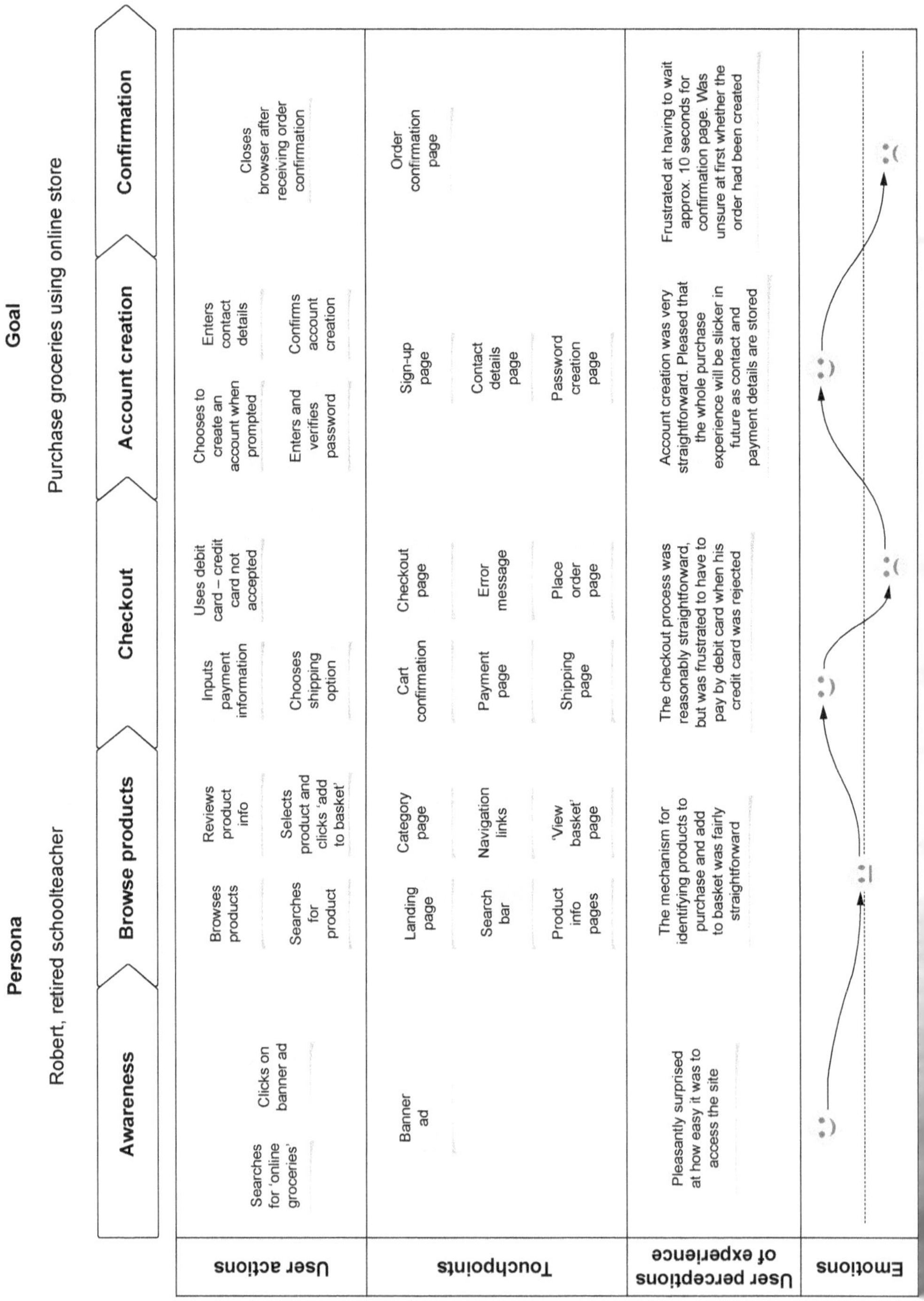

Persona
Robert, retired schoolteacher

Goal
Purchase groceries using online store

	Awareness	Browse products	Checkout	Account creation	Confirmation
User actions	Searches for 'online groceries' — Clicks on banner ad	Browses products — Reviews product info — Searches for product — Selects product and clicks 'add to basket'	Inputs payment information — Uses debit card – credit card not accepted — Chooses shipping option	Chooses to create an account when prompted — Enters contact details — Enters and verifies password — Confirms account creation	Closes browser after receiving order confirmation
Touchpoints	Banner ad	Landing page — Category page — Search bar — Navigation links — Product info pages — 'View basket' page	Cart confirmation — Checkout page — Payment page — Error message — Shipping page — Place order page	Sign-up page — Contact details page — Password creation page	Order confirmation page
User perceptions of experience	Pleasantly surprised at how easy it was to access the site	The mechanism for identifying products to purchase and add to basket was fairly straightforward	The checkout process was reasonably straightforward, but was frustrated to have to pay by debit card when his credit card was rejected	Account creation was very straightforward. Pleased that the whole purchase experience will be slicker in future as contact and payment details are stored	Frustrated at having to wait approx. 10 seconds for confirmation page. Was unsure at first whether the order had been created
Emotions	:)	:|	:)	:)	:(

4   PROCESS DESIGN

INTRODUCTION

As with all other digital solution design activities, when designing the processes within a digital solution, the designer needs to ensure the design objectives introduced in Table 1.1 are being achieved. In the context of process design, arguably the most critical objective is functional correctness and completeness. Consequently, the principal objective of process design is:

> To specify how the functional requirements defined during Requirements Engineering will be realised using a series of individual programs, components or services, that will be built and will interact with each other in order to deliver the required solution behaviour.

The concepts of logical and physical design were introduced in Chapter 2, and these relate to all aspects of design. In the context of process design, when considering the logical design of processes, decisions made about which programs, components and services are required, and how these interact with each other to realise the required functionality, are agnostic of the technology that is used. Physical process design, however, will specify which technologies are used to build those programs, components and services, and the specific protocols used to pass messages between them.

In addition to specifying how the required functionality is to be realised, the designer also needs to consider how the other design objectives introduced in Chapter 1, such as the need to produce reusable code and the desire for an efficient, reliable, expandable and maintainable solution, will be achieved.

As with I/O design, the start point for process design is the documentation from the analysis work undertaken by the business/system analyst(s), such as a Business Requirements Document (BRD), which includes a requirements catalogue, or a solution backlog and accompanying models, such as a use case model and a class model, representing the required functionality and data, respectively.

The UML use case diagram in Figure 3.1 identifies five key system processes to be specified, one for each use case:

- Place Order;
- Pick Order;

- Despatch Order;
- Record Delivery;
- Raise Invoice.

Although, theoretically, logical process design would be undertaken before considering physical process design, in practice the approach that the designer takes from here typically depends on the target environment that the solution will be deployed in. For instance, if the solution is a standalone app that will execute within a smart device (such as a smartphone, tablet or watch) or a desktop app running on a laptop or desktop PC with no network connectivity required, then the design can be relatively straightforward and the designer may skip logical design and jump straight to physical design. But if the target environment is a series of networked geographically dispersed workstations, with mobile users requiring access from their laptops, tablet PCs, smartphones, smart watches or an IoT smart device, then the task becomes significantly more complex and the designer may choose to undertake logical design prior to specifying platform-specific designs.

PROCESS DESIGN STAGES

Process design is performed at two levels:

- **Solution-level design**: This is concerned with identifying the discrete software components and services needed to realise the functional requirements, and the interfaces necessary to enable them to communicate with each other. This activity corresponds to the *solution design* stage in the V model software development life cycle (SDLC). The V model was introduced in Book 1 and has been reproduced in Figure 4.1

Figure 4.1 V model SDLC

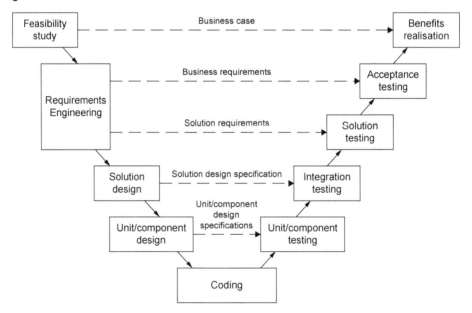

- **Unit-, component- or service-level design** (referred to simply as unit design herein): This defines how each program, component or service identified in the solution-level design is to be built. This activity (also referred to as module design, component engineering or service design) corresponds to the *unit/component design* stage in the V model SDLC.

In practice, these levels also equate to stages in the design process. Solution-level design must be undertaken before unit design can begin. However, it is common for designers to revisit the solution-level design as the unit design progresses, and hence, the process becomes iterative, especially during Agile developments.

KEY CONSTRUCTS IN PROCESS SPECIFICATION

Software processes – indeed, all processes – are created from three basic constructs:

- **Sequence**: The steps in this construct are executed in sequence. The sequence never changes and all steps are executed every time the construct is executed.

- **Selection**: The steps in this construct are selectively executed dependent on certain conditions. This leads to alternative paths being taken based on whether a condition is true or false.

- **Iteration**: The steps in this construct are executed multiple times (or sometimes not at all) depending on some condition being true. These constructs are commonly referred to as loops because the process loops back and repeats one or more steps. There are different types of iteration (loop). Some test the condition before performing the iteration steps and others test the condition after performing the iteration steps. With the former, if the loop condition is false when first tested, the iteration steps will never be executed. With the latter, the iteration steps will always be performed at least once. A third type of iteration repeats a predetermined number of times, or for each occurrence of some data (e.g. for each order item).

All programming languages support these three basic constructs, so software developers can easily translate the design into source code to build the working software.

STEPWISE REFINEMENT

Stepwise refinement refers to a particular approach to specifying processes. It can either be conducted in a top-down fashion or a bottom-up fashion.

Top-down stepwise refinement starts with a high-level overview of the process (or system), which identifies a set of high-level units (modules, components or services). Each of these is then decomposed into a more detailed set of subprocesses or units, and the approach continues until the desired level of specification is achieved.

With **bottom-up stepwise refinement** (a less common approach), a set of base elements of the process or system are specified first, in detail, and these elements are then linked together to form larger subsystems, which are then linked – sometimes in many levels – until a complete top-level process or solution is formed.

COUPLING AND COHESION

When identifying and defining the components and services that make up a digital solution, the designer must consider the principles of good modular design, such as reusability and maintainability. Both of these principles are addressed by two design concepts, coupling and cohesion, which place constraints upon the components and services (modules) by requiring them to be **loosely coupled** and **highly cohesive**.

Coupling is essentially a measure of the independence of the modules within a solution. Loosely coupled modules are relatively independent of one another, which means that one module can be modified with little or no impact on any other modules. However, there must always be some degree of coupling – and hence dependency – between two modules if one uses the services provided by the other. In component-based design (CBD, see example 2 below), the concept of an interface is the mechanism designers use to achieve loose coupling.

Cohesion is a measure of how closely related the aspects of a module are to each other. A module should have a well-defined role (or purpose) within the solution and carry out a single problem-related function. Therefore, the designer breaks down a module that is not cohesive (covers more than one function) into a set of more 'single-minded' sub-modules until all of the lowest level modules perform only one, well-defined function. This is the concept of top-down stepwise refinement, introduced above.

In general, loosely coupled, highly cohesive modules can be more easily reused, and reusability is a key design objective for most products, including digital solutions. Using a module (component/service) that already exists achieves the following benefits:

- **Reduces development time** as the program code has already been written.

- **Reduces risk**, assuming that the module is already tried and tested, and hence reliable.

- **Supports standardisation** as reusing a module in multiple places/solutions increases consistency as the outcome (in terms of behaviour, look and feel) will always be the same.

PROCESS DESIGN EXAMPLES

The approach to process design varies depending on the design paradigm used. Chapter 2 introduced four popular software design paradigms: monolithic, component-based, service-oriented and domain-driven. Detailed coverage of how process design would be approached for each of these paradigms is beyond the scope of this book. Instead, the remainder of this chapter focuses on monolithic and component-based, which also includes the techniques applicable to the others. The service-oriented paradigm is covered further in Chapter 7 in the context of software architecture, as it is also a software architecture pattern.

Example 1: Monolithic design

Monolithic design is typically employed for uncomplicated digital solutions, such as a standalone, single-user PC-based or smartphone application. With monolithic design the solution is typically developed as a single executable software component, executing on a single device. In this situation the high-level design may focus on a set of individual modules (also referred to as subroutines or functions) that are linked together to form a single executable program. Figure 4.2 shows the high-level (solution) design for a straightforward standalone application, in the form of a basic module chart.

Figure 4.2 Basic module chart for a standalone application

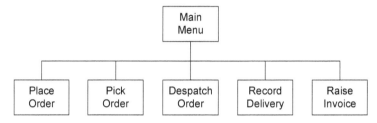

Having identified the high-level program modules, the designer continues to specify each one in more detail, using stepwise refinement. Figure 4.3 shows a UML activity diagram, which defines the high-level algorithm used to specify the decomposition of the Place Order function.

Each box in Figure 4.3 represents a sub-task in the Place Order process. The ⌐⌐ symbol denotes that the task is further defined in a lower-level activity diagram (not included here). This is an example of unit design.

The algorithm defined in Figure 4.3 incorporates all three process constructs described above. First, the entire diagram represents a **sequence** of tasks that make up the process. **Selection** constructs begin with a **decision** (denoted by a diamond symbol with one arrow pointing towards the diamond and two or more arrows pointing away from the diamond, each representing an alternative path that is executed when the corresponding **guard condition** (denoted by the use of square brackets next to the relevant line) is true). For example, when the condition [new customer] is true, the process continues with the task Enter customer details, but when the condition [existing customer] is true, the process continues with the task Confirm customer details. The task Add item to basket represents an **iteration** (loop) construct, as the task is repeated while the condition [more items to order] is true. As the loop condition has been placed after the repeated task, the task will always be performed at least once, ensuring that the order will comprise at least one item. The diamond preceding the task Add item to basket represents the merging of the two alternative paths, and not a decision, as there are multiple paths entering the diamond and only one path exiting it, whereas with decisions, there would be only one path entering the diamond and multiple paths exiting it.

Example 2: Component-based design

While the use of a basic module chart and process flowcharts (activity diagrams) built using stepwise refinement might be sufficient for straightforward standalone applications (monolithic applications), this approach is too simplistic when designing processes in any application that requires the integration of a series of components in order to realise the required functionality.

Figure 4.3 UML activity diagram: decomposition of the Place Order process

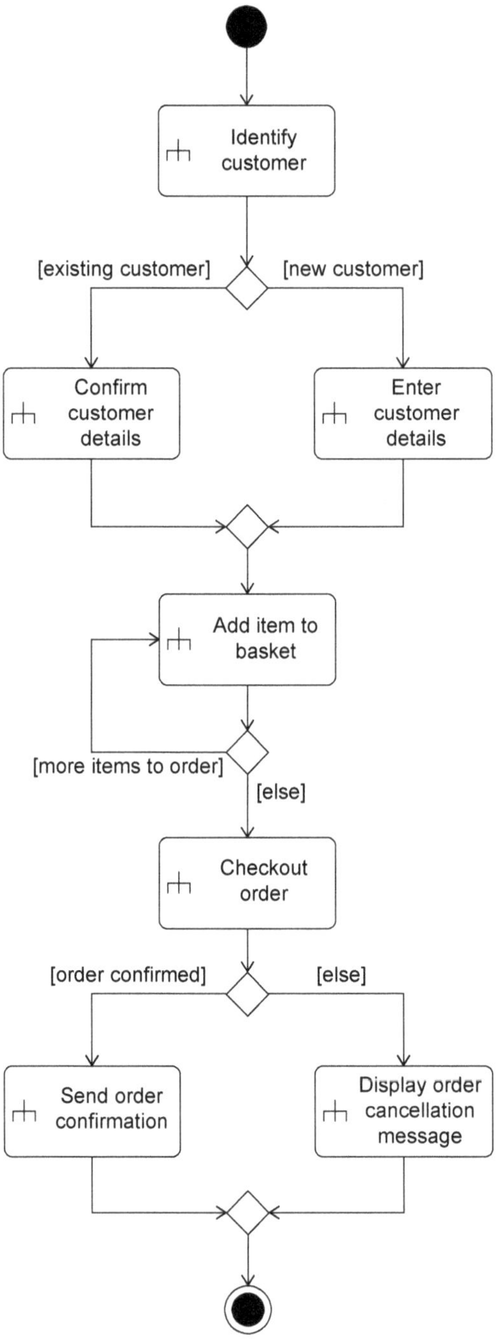

With CBD, process design involves four key stages:

1. Identify the components needed to realise the requirements.

2. Determine how these components need to interact with each other.

3. Define the required component interfaces.

4. Specify how each component will realise each service exposed within the component's interface(s).

Identifying components

When undertaking solution-level design using a component-based approach, the components can be treated as 'black boxes'. That is to say, at this stage the focus is on what services a component needs to provide, and what services (provided by other components) the component depends on, in order to provide those services. It is not necessary to understand how those services are realised by the components, as this is achieved during stage 4 (unit/component design).

Treating components as black boxes helps to achieve the concept of **encapsulation**, where certain contents of a component are hidden, or protected, within the component, and hence cannot be accessed directly or changed by another component. The only aspect of the component that is visible to other components is the **interface** (or application programming interface (API)), which exposes the services provided by the component.

Components can be acquired from a variety of sources – they can be purchased off-the-shelf from a commercial off-the-shelf (COTS) vendor or marketplace (such as ComponentSource® – see componentsource.com), reused from an in-house component library, obtained as open-source software, or custom-built from scratch to meet the needs of a particular solution.

Figure 4.4 shows part of a solution-level design in the form of a UML component diagram. The solution is made up of three components: a smartphone app, a website and a back-end system. The app and website use services provided by the back-end Order Management System, indicated by the **required and provided interfaces**; the former indicated by the ⊃ symbol and the latter by the ◯ symbol. The dashed lines show that the Smartphone App and Website have a dependency on the interface iOrderManagement, provided by the Order Management System. This diagram represents a logical design as it makes no mention of any technology specifics.

When deciding which components will be needed within a solution, the designer ensures that each component has a single, clear purpose within the overall solution, and a set of services provided by the component that are logically connected. How the designer decides on the cohesive grouping of services is beyond the scope of this book, but one approach (**conceptual cohesion**) groups services based on a particular underlying concept.

Determining how components interact

Having identified which components will be needed within the solution, the next logical step is to determine how the components need to interact with each other in order

Figure 4.4 UML component diagram: solution-level design

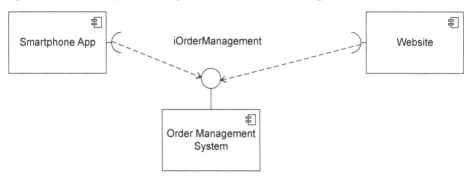

to realise the desired functionality. The required functionality will typically have been specified by a business analyst (BA) during Requirements Engineering, either as a use case or a user story. Figure 4.5 shows the main scenario for a use case Place Order, which defines a function that will be available from both the Smartphone App and the Website. The use case description shown in Figure 4.5 uses the structured narrative style introduced by Alistair Cockburn (2001).

Figure 4.5 Use case extract: Place Order function

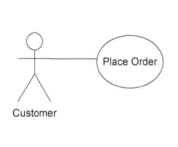

Customer

Use case/goal	Place Order
Scope	Order Management System
Actor	Customer
Preconditions	Customer has pre-registered and is logged in to the Smartphone App or Website
Success guarantees	New order created and confirmation email sent to customer
Main success scenario	1. System displays customer details and requests confirmation 2. Actor confirms details 3. Actor adds item to basket 4. Repeat step 3 until no more items to add 5. Actor requests checkout 6. System invokes Checkout Order 7. System creates new order and sends order confirmation 8. Use case ends

Using the use case description and component diagram, the designer can create an interaction diagram – most commonly a UML sequence diagram – to illustrate the interactions required between the components to achieve the functionality specified in the use case description. Figure 4.6 presents a UML sequence diagram derived from the component diagram and use case description shown in Figures 4.4 and 4.5.

Determining component interfaces

Modelling the interactions between components using diagrams such as the sequence diagram in Figure 4.6 identifies the messages that need to be passed between components in order to invoke services. Other than the messages being sent from the actor to the Smartphone App, all of the messages are being sent from the Smartphone App to the Order Management System, which indicates that the Smartphone App is

Figure 4.6 UML sequence diagram: Place Order use case realisation

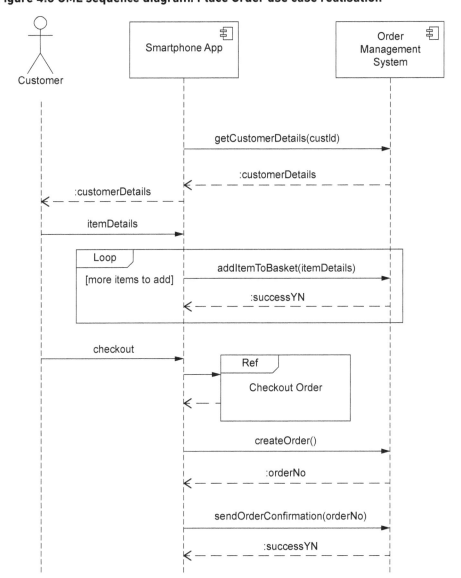

invoking services provided by the Order Management System. This is also indicated by the dependency arrow from the Smartphone App to the Order Management System in the component diagram in Figure 4.4. The individual messages being sent to the Order Management System are:

- getCustomerDetails;
- addItemToBasket;

- createOrder;

- sendOrderConfirmation.

In Figure 4.4, the interface provided by the component Order Management System was identified as iOrderManagement. This interface can now be defined using the UML class diagram notation (an interface being a special kind of class in UML), as shown in Figure 4.7.

Figure 4.7 UML class diagram: iOrderManagement interface definition

<<interface>> iOrderManagement
+ getCustomerDetails(custId) : customerDetails + addItemToBasket(itemDetails) : successYN + createOrder() : orderNo + sendOrderConfirmation(orderNo) : successYN

Figure 4.7 shows four services that are provided by the Order Management System component. Notice that the name of the service corresponds to the name shown on the corresponding message in Figure 4.6. The + symbol that precedes each service indicates that the service is public, which means that it is visible to other components.

The definition of each message comprises three elements:

- **Service name**: Corresponds to the name used for the message within an interaction diagram to invoke the service. For example, getCustomerDetails, addItemToBasket, createOrder, sendOrderConfirmation.

- **Parameters**: Also referred to as 'arguments', this part of the message defines one or more distinct pieces of data that can be passed to the service to influence how the service behaves, for example custId, itemDetails, orderNo. Figure 4.6 shows two examples of where a single discrete value is passed to the service (custId and orderNo); the third (itemDetails) is an example of what is referred to as a user-defined data type, a data structure containing multiple discrete values.

- **Return type**: Identifies the data type of the value(s) returned by the service to the requesting component. For example, customerDetails, orderNo, successYN. As with parameters, return types can either take the form of a single discrete value (successYN, orderNo) or a more complex data structure (customerDetails).

During the design process the designer often needs to define a data structure that can be passed back and forth between components or services. In Figure 4.7, itemDetails as a parameter comprises a set of discrete data values rather than a single value. Similarly with customerDetails as a return type. Sometimes this can simply be shown using the data type xml, which denotes an XML schema defined separately, such as:

```
getCustomerDetails(custId) : xml
```

However, this is not particularly meaningful. So, instead, the designer can create their own data type classifier using class model elements, which they can then refer to explicitly, as in Figure 4.7, which is more meaningful to the reader. Figure 4.8 shows the definition of the data type classifier `CustomerDetails`.

Figure 4.8 UML data type classifier: CustomerDetails

```
┌─────────────────────────────┐
│        <<datatype>>         │
│       CustomerDetails       │
├─────────────────────────────┤
│ custId : string             │
│ name : string               │
│ address : Address           │
│ phone : string              │
│ email : string              │
│ creditLimit : int           │
│                             │
└─────────────────────────────┘
```

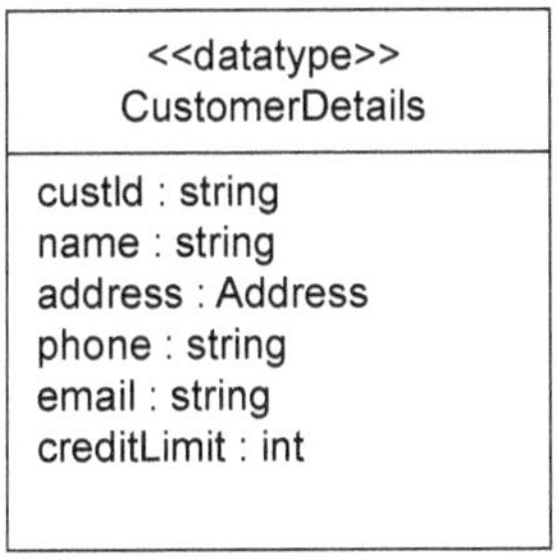

Figure 4.8 shows that the data type `CustomerDetails` comprises six discrete values (`custId`, `name`, `address`, `phone`, `email` and `creditLimit`), each with their own data type (`string`, `Address` or `int`). `string` and `int` are standard, discrete data types in UML. `string` data values can be made up of any combination of alphanumeric characters. `int` data values must contain a valid integer number. However, `Address` is itself a data type created by the designer, which would, in turn, have its own data type classifier.

In software engineering, an interface supports the core design principle of loose coupling by reducing dependencies between components. When one component (for example Component A) relies on services from another component (Component B), Component A depends on the interface provided by Component B rather than its specific internal code. Component B implements this interface using its own program code, which can evolve over time without affecting Component A, provided the interface definition remains unchanged. The interface definition (see example in Figure 4.7) establishes a contract or set of rules that dictate how software components interact, specifying the services a component must provide without detailing how those services are implemented. This approach provides the flexibility to modify the implementation of a service without impacting the components that are dependent on the interface. In some cases, designers may choose to offer multiple implementations of the same interface, as shown in Figure 4.9, which demonstrates an implementation of the adapter design pattern introduced in Chapter 2.

In Figure 4.9, the component `Client` has a dependency on the interface `iDatabaseAdapter`, which is implemented (realised) by three separate components: `Oracle23aiAdapter`, `DB2Adapter` and `SQLServerAdapter`, each of which provides a technology-specific implementation of the two services `getConnection` and `runQuery`. The ellipsis symbol (...) is not part of the UML notation, but is used to show that the list of services is incomplete (in the interests of simplifying the example), as it is likely to include other services not shown.

Figure 4.9 UML class diagram extract: database adapter

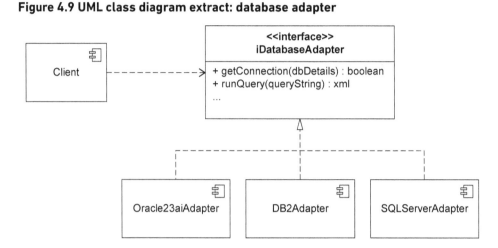

Specifying how components realise their interfaces (designing the services)

The above sections have discussed the high-level solution design, which identifies which components are required, how the components interact with each other to realise the requirements, and what interfaces and services are required to support those interactions. The designer then turns their attention to how each component realises each interface and service, to enable a developer to build the components using program code.

A common approach is to create a 'class' in code (most modern programming languages are object-oriented, and hence support the class concept) with the same operation names as the names of the services in the interface. It is common practice to name the class with the suffix 'Manager', as the class essentially manages the internal workings of the component to realise each service provided via the interface.

Then, using interaction modelling, the designer specifies for each operation the required interactions with the other classes in the component. Figure 4.10 shows a subset of the design-level classes for the Order Management System component.

In Figure 4.10 the class OrderManager has been created to realise the interface iOrderManagement (denoted by the dashed arrow with the triangular arrowhead). An additional class (DataManager) has been created to handle any communication with the persistent data storage technology, assuming that the data storage mechanism is some database that accepts queries to manipulate the data. Again, the ellipses (...) in the diagram indicate that these are partial entries, so each class (including the interface) will potentially have additional attributes and operations/services.

In essence, the OrderManager class realises the interface as follows:

- When a message is sent to the OrderManagementSystem component, the operation within the OrderManager object with the same name as the message is

Figure 4.10 UML class diagram: design-level classes for the Order Management System component

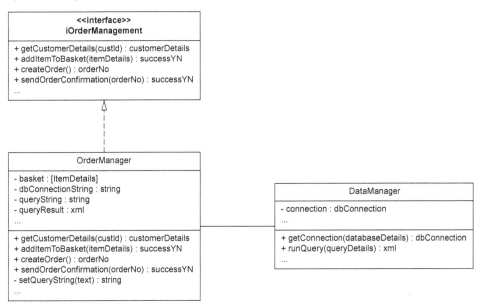

invoked, and the program code that sits behind the operation is executed.[10] These operations are sometimes referred to as 'handlers', as they handle the messages received by the component.

- The first thing that happens within each of the 'handler' operations is to send a message to the DataManager object, invoking its getConnection operation to establish a connection with the database containing the required data.

- Then, depending on the service being realised, the corresponding handler operation creates the necessary query string to be sent to the database to retrieve the required data. The format of the query string will depend on the database technology being used; a common approach is to use Structured Query Language (SQL), which is supported by most popular database management systems (DBMSs).

- The handler operation then sends a message to the DataManager object to invoke its runQuery operation, which, in turn, requests the DBMS to run the query, passing the query string it received from the OrderManager object to the DBMS via the DBMS' own API. When the DBMS receives the message from the DataManager object, it executes the query to extract the required data and returns an xml data structure (dataset) containing the results of the query.

- Finally, the DataManager object's runQuery operation returns the xml data structure to the OrderManager object's handler operation, which in turn packages up the data into the format required by the handler's return type and passes it back to the 'client' component (the component that invoked the service originally).

---

10 The code that realises an operation is often called the method.

The interaction described above is shown in the UML sequence diagram in Figure 4.11, which essentially describes the internal workings of the OrderManager object's getCustomerDetails handler operation. The interaction between the DataManager object and the DBMS API is not shown on the diagram because that would be part of the DataManager's runQuery operation, which would be defined in a separate interaction diagram.

Figure 4.11 UML sequence diagram: realisation of getCustomerDetails service

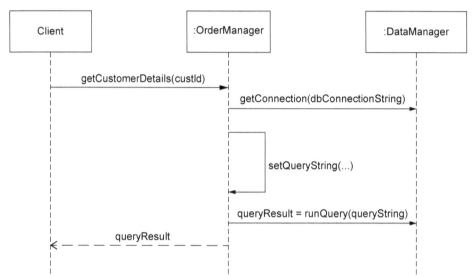

Note that Figure 4.11 includes a **reflexive message** (setQueryString), which is a message from the OrderManager object to itself. This is because the implementation of the operation getCustomerDetails needs to invoke the operation setQueryString prior to sending the runQuery message to the DataManager object. Note that in Figure 4.10 the setQueryString operation in the OrderManager class is private (denoted by the minus symbol preceding the operation name). This indicates that the operation is only visible (and hence accessible) within the OrderManager object itself, and cannot be invoked by any other object.

5 DATA DESIGN

INTRODUCTION

Data is the lifeblood of digital solutions, so data design is a critical activity within digital solution design. The principal objective of data design is:

> To define a set of flexible data structures that will enable the realisation of the functional and non-functional requirements agreed during Requirements Engineering, by supporting the input, output and process designs.

The start point for data design is often a model of the data requirements, or a high-level business domain model, typically in the form of a UML class diagram or an entity–relationship diagram (ERD). If no such analysis model is available, then the designer needs to start by producing their own model. This can be achieved by identifying classes (or entities) from the requirements documentation or solution backlog. A detailed description of this process is outside the scope of this book.

Although an 'analysis' data model is a good starting point for data design, the model is typically not in a suitable format to enable a robust set of data structures to be created within the target hardware and software environment. This is because, during the analysis stage of a solution development project, the BA (or system analyst) produces a high-level conceptual data model that reflects the kinds of data that the organisation is interested in and is needed to support the functional requirements. However, this 'analysis' model usually only contains a subset of the data required to support a coherent digital solution, and is often missing key data attributes and relationships between the logical data structures (entities/classes). Therefore, the designer must take this analysis model and extend it to form a comprehensive design-level data model that can be used by a developer or database specialist when developing the physical data structures, based on the use of appropriate data technologies.

Before considering some of the key techniques and technologies involved in data design, it is first necessary to introduce some key concepts.

KEY CONCEPTS IN DATA DESIGN

Data, information and information systems

Many people use the terms data and information interchangeably, but it can be useful to understand the distinction between them.

Keith Gordon, in his book *Modelling Business Information: Entity Relationship and Class Modelling for Business Analysts* (Gordon, 2017), grapples with the two terms by starting with a common explanation of the difference between data and information:

> [*data* is] facts, events, transactions and similar that have been recorded [and *information* is] data in context or data that has been processed and communicated so that it can be used by its recipient.

He continues to provide a more meaningful definition:

> a re-interpretable representation of information in a formalised manner suitable for communication, interpretation or processing

which he visualises in the diagram in Figure 5.1.

Figure 5.1 The relationship between data and information (© BCS, The Chartered Institute for IT)

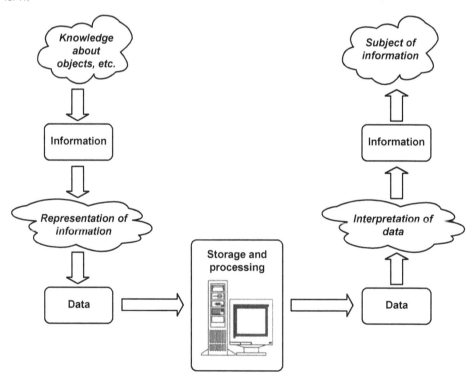

Most technical stakeholders involved in digital solution development tend to focus their attention on data, while business stakeholders focus their attention on information, with BAs often translating and mapping between the two.

With regard to information systems, at least in the context of this book, an information system can be seen as:

> a digital solution that stores and processes data to deliver meaningful information to its target users.

Data at rest and data in transit

When designing datasets to be stored and processed by a digital solution, it is important to consider both data at rest and data in transit.

Data at rest refers to the persistent storage of data for subsequent use. For example, when a customer registers their account details on a website, those details must be stored in some form of permanent storage so that they do not disappear as soon as the customer leaves the website. This means that, when the customer returns to the website at a later time, perhaps to place an order or book a ticket, their details can be retrieved from the persistent data store rather than the customer having to re-enter them.

Data in transit, as the name suggests, refers to data that is being transmitted between separate components or applications. For example, in the component diagram in Figure 4.4, the `Order Management System` component provides a set of services to the `Smartphone App` and `Website` via the interface `iOrderManagement`. When a service provided by the `Order Management System` is invoked, data will typically be transmitted across some network between the `Smartphone App` or the `Website` (or both) and the `Order Management System`. The format of this data will need to be designed just like the format of the permanent storage of the customer details mentioned above.

Since it is not actively being transmitted, data at rest is generally considered less vulnerable to interception. However, hackers can still target data at rest through malware or by gaining access to storage devices. In contrast, data in transit, because it is being transferred across a network, like the internet or a local network connection, is often more vulnerable to being intercepted by hackers, and data breaches often target data in transit. Chapter 6 explores some of the security vulnerabilities and protection mechanisms that can be deployed to protect both data at rest and data in transit.

Structured, unstructured and semi-structured data

Another key consideration during data design is the nature of the data. In general, data can exist in two fundamental forms: 'structured' and 'unstructured'. These terms refer to the format and organisation of data and inform the way it is managed and used.

Distinguishing between structured and unstructured data is important because of the limitations of certain technologies when it comes to their ability to handle such data.

Until recent developments in data science (2010 onwards) and the introduction of related technologies, certain data capabilities have only been possible with structured data, notably to perform significant data analytics on the data content. However, many organisations need to deal with huge volumes of data (often referred to as **big data**) in order to manage complex real-time applications and derive insights from increasingly complex business environments.

Structured data

Structured data is stored with a high degree of organisation, where data types, formats and relationships are explicitly defined, with data typically existing in a tabular form consisting of columns (fields or attributes) and rows (records), as per the example in Figure 5.2.

Figure 5.2 Example of structured data in tabular form

SaleID	Name	Product	Value
123	Pete	CD	5.00
234	Meg	Record	15.00
345	Toby	Book	20.00

The definitions (called schemas) of each data structure determine the rules that the data held in that structure must follow. This includes the format of data stored in each column as well as whether a column must contain a value (in other words, is mandatory) for each record. The structure that is formed is usually referred to as a table, and this supports the ability to identify particular rows, or records, within that table and to access particular values stored in the columns, or attributes, of each row. Implicit in the use of such schema-driven structures is the high degree of consistency, which essentially means that:

- records in a table store data about the same kind of thing, determinable from the table name (e.g. Customer or Order); and
- data held in a column or attribute of a table have the same meaning, determinable from the attribute or column name (e.g. customerID or orderDate).

In addition to the high degree of data consistency, the rigid structure is perfectly suited to analysis and relational modelling (explained later in this chapter), and is more accessible to a wider range of users, due to the easy-to-understand tabular format.

In practice, digital solutions usually require a number of structured tables. For example:

- a table of order information and a table of customer information in a sales order processing system;

- a table of employee records and a table of job descriptions in an HR system; and

- a table of product data and a table of stock data for an inventory management system.

These tables are linked meaningfully using a referencing mechanism. The tables and their links are typically stored in a **database**, which is maintained by a generic data management application called a database management system (DBMS), or by purpose-built programs manipulating data files containing tables. Both methods ensure conformance of the stored data to the structured schema.

Structured data is well suited to supporting the day-to-day operational needs of an enterprise where individual data records are constantly being created, retrieved and updated. This is often referred to as **online transaction processing** (OLTP). However, where the data needs to be filtered, aggregated, grouped and sorted for reporting and analytical purposes (**online analytical processing** (OLAP)), its rigid structure can be a barrier, which leads to poor performance and unnecessarily complex, time-consuming and costly preprocessing.

Changes to some databases can be complex due to their relational[11] nature, and the fact that formats are predefined and rigid. This can be a blocker to fast exploratory analysis and development. Development and maintenance of structured data can be costly as there is generally a significant amount of design work and data warehouse (see data technologies later in this chapter) development needed to start, and the cost of queries and scaling data warehouses, particularly on a cloud solution, can quickly build.

In terms of manipulating structured data, Structured Query Language (SQL) is the language that is used to query the data, manipulate the structure of the data and build repeatable common tasks in the form of stored procedures and views. SQL is a fairly basic language that is widely used across many structured database tools such as SQL Server, MySQL, PostgreSQL and Oracle, and although there are variations in dialects, it is largely consistent.

Unstructured data

Unstructured data is characterised by its lack of a predefined format or organisation. The data typically remains in its native form without any formatting to aid interpretation, as can be seen in Figure 5.3, which shows an unstructured equivalent of the tabular data in Figure 5.2.

Figure 5.3 An example of unstructured data

> There are 3 sales, ID 123 is an order to the value of £5.00 for Pete, he has ordered a CD. Meg has ordered a Record for £15.00 under order ID 234 and Toby has placed order 345 for a £20.00 book.

Unstructured data does not lend itself to data modelling, which limits its usefulness. In particular, challenges arise when such data needs to be processed and used in another application, for example an analytical (OLAP) solution. This is due to the data being in a

---

11 Relational refers to relational theory, which governs the structure of SQL/relational databases.

raw native format, which requires specialist tooling and expertise to process and extract useful insights.

Despite the challenges in analysing unstructured data, it can be beneficial for certain uses, as the data can be stored at scale in a **data lake** or **data lakehouse**, enabling fast data collection and ingestion, and rapid growth of data volumes. Generally these are more cost-effective options than storing the data in databases, due to the simplicity and scale of storage they offer.

Large language models (LLMs) and machine learning (ML) can aid the extraction of valuable insights from unstructured data such as text, images or audio, by leveraging advanced algorithms and natural language processing (NLP). LLMs, such as Generative Pre-trained Transformer (GPT), process and understand human language to identify patterns, summarise information, classify content and answer queries. ML models analyse unstructured data to detect trends, categorise information and generate predictions. Together, they can convert unstructured data into structured insights, helping in tasks such as sentiment analysis, topic modelling, entity recognition and customer feedback interpretation, thus driving informed decision-making.

Common examples of unstructured data include:

- **text documents**, such as emails, letters, reports, presentations, social media posts;
- **multimedia**, such as images, videos and audio files, which are encoded using specific codecs (such as MP3, AAC, FLAC and ALAC for audio and MP4, AVI and MKV for video);
- **web pages**, comprising the text, images and videos on a page; while the HTML code provides some structure, the content itself is not organised in a way that allows for easy analysis;
- **sensor data** from devices such as smartphones and smartwatches, which collect large volumes of data about the user's activity and surroundings, including things like GPS coordinates, accelerometer readings and microphone recordings; and
- **customer feedback**, where open-ended survey responses, reviews and social media comments contain valuable insights but require special techniques to analyse.

While some unstructured data can be reformatted or interpreted using AI technologies (such as NLP and ML), to derive valuable insights, others must remain in their unstructured format (e.g. image, audio and video files), as these 'unstructured' formats are necessary to encode media content, and are decoded by specialist media viewer/player applications.

Semi-structured data
Semi-structured data is a hybrid between fully structured data and unstructured data. It offers more organisation than unstructured data but doesn't conform to the rigid schemas of traditional databases.

Unlike structured data in tables with predefined columns, semi-structured data has its own internal organisation, and is often stored in a JavaScript Object Notation (JSON) or XML file. These formats use tags and other markers to infer a typically hierarchical structure rather than adhering to a strict tabular form defined in a schema. Figure 5.4 shows a semi-structured equivalent of the tabular data from Figure 5.2.

Figure 5.4 An example of semi-structured data

```
{
  "name": "Sales",
  "records": [
    {
      "id": 123,
      "name": "Pete",
      "product": "CD",
      "value": 5
    },
    {
      "id": 234,
      "name": "Meg",
      "product": "Record",
      "value": 15
    },
    {
      "id": 345,
      "name": "Toby",
      "product": "Book",
      "value": 20   }
  ]
}
```

The beauty of semi-structured data is its adaptability. The structure can vary to accommodate different types of information without needing a fixed format. The flexible structure allows for incorporating new data types or elements without breaking the entire system, which represents a more agile, scalable and cost-effective storage method than structured databases. Additionally, compared to unstructured data, semi-structured data's inherent organisation makes it easier to process. Consequently, many modern applications and data sources generate or use semi-structured data.

However, while offering more structure than unstructured data, semi-structured data can still be complex to analyse because it is not possible to access the data using simple SQL queries, as with a schema-based database. The inherent flexibility can also lead to inconsistencies in how data is organised, potentially impacting data quality.

Common examples of semi-structured data include:

- **emails**, which contain both structured (sender, recipient, subject, date) and unstructured data (the body content and attachments);

- **log files**, which often contain a mix of structured data (timestamps) and unstructured data (log messages) – server log files, for example, contain records of user activity or system events, including timestamps, Internet Protocol (IP) addresses and descriptions of actions, but the format can vary depending on the application;

- **sensor data**, where devices such as fitness trackers or smart thermostats generate sensor data that often includes timestamps and sensor readings (heart rate, temperature), but the specific format might differ between devices;

- **web pages** – although HTML provides structure with tags, web pages can be semi-structured due to the inclusion of text, images and multimedia elements laid out in various ways; and

- **social media posts**, which typically contain a combination of text, hashtags and mentions, along with timestamps and user information – the specific structure can vary depending on the platform.

Qualitative versus quantitative data

The distinction between qualitative and quantitative data is arguably more relevant to the BA than to the data designer, as this will have a bearing on the data requirements for a digital solution to meet a particular business need. However, these two fundamental types of data will also have a bearing on what kind of data a digital solution needs to capture, and how it is collected, stored, processed and analysed. Digital solutions often require a mix of quantitative and qualitative data.

Quantitative data
Quantitative data refers to numeric or measurable information used to answer questions such as 'how many?' ('How many people visited our website last week?'), 'how much?' ('How much was the average customer review rating for a product?' or 'How much was the total sales value last month?'), or 'how often?' ('How often does a customer place an order?').

Quantitative data is typically collected through structured methods such as surveys, experiments or sensors that record numerical information. It is valuable for identifying patterns, tracking trends, comparing groups and testing hypotheses due to its clear, measurable nature. However, it may lack the context or deeper insights behind the numbers.

Qualitative data
Qualitative data consists of descriptive information that focuses on understanding 'why', offering valuable insights into people's experiences, motivations and the context behind the 'how' questions mentioned earlier. It captures perspectives, opinions and emotions through sources such as interviews, open-ended survey responses and customer reviews, which are analysed thematically to identify recurring ideas, patterns and meanings. While qualitative data provides depth and context, it can be subjective and may not be easily generalised to larger populations.

Big data

Big data refers to extremely large and diverse collections of data that grow at ever-increasing rates. These datasets are so voluminous and complex, and arrive so rapidly, that traditional data processing software is unable to manage them efficiently.

Big data is characterised by:

- **Volume**: The amount of data is immense. Datasets can range from terabytes to zettabytes, and continue to grow exponentially. See Table 5.1 for a comparison of data storage sizes to get a sense of just how big this is.

Table 5.1 Common data storage sizes

Unit	Abbreviation	Size
Byte	B	1 byte
Kilobyte	KB	1,024 bytes
Megabyte	MB	1,048,576 bytes
Gigabyte	GB	1,073,741,824 bytes
Terabyte	TB	1,099,511,627,776 bytes
Petabyte	PB	1,024 terabytes
Exabyte	EB	1,024 petabytes
Zettabyte	ZB	1,024 exabytes

- **Variety**: The data comes in many forms, including structured data (traditional databases), unstructured data (text, social media posts, images, videos, sensor data) and semi-structured data (log files, emails).

- **Velocity**: The speed at which data is generated and collected is constantly increasing. Social media activity, sensor networks, machine-generated data and internet traffic all contribute to the ever-growing data stream.

These characteristics pose challenges for traditional data management systems:

- **Storage and processing**: Traditional data storage and processing systems struggle to keep up with the volume and ingestion rate of big data.

- **Analysis**: Extracting meaningful insights from massive and diverse datasets requires specialised tools and techniques.

However, big data also brings significant opportunities:

- **Improved decision-making**: Analysis of big data enables businesses to gain deeper insights into the behaviour of customers and the day-to-day operation of their business, leading to data-driven decisions that can optimise business operations and provide a competitive advantage.

- **Real-time analytics**: The high velocity of big data allows for real-time analysis and near-instant decision-making based on the latest information, rather than traditional periodic (weekly, monthly, quarterly and annual) management reporting cycles.

- **Innovation**: Big data can fuel innovation in various fields, from scientific research and healthcare to personalised marketing and product development.

Master data, reference data and transactional data

Master data, reference data and transactional data are all important parts of an organisation's data ecosystem, each with its own distinct purpose:

- **Master data**: Core, foundational information about key entities within a business that is consistent across departments and applications, providing a single source of truth. For example:
  - customer data (names, addresses, contact details);
  - product data (descriptions, prices, inventory levels);
  - supplier data (names, contact information, payment terms); and
  - employee data (names, addresses, salaries, job titles).
- **Reference data**: Defines standardised values or classifications used to categorise or contextualise master data. Reference data is relatively static (remains constant and does not change over time or in response to user actions or system processes) and often includes predefined codes or values, which helps to ensure consistency and standardisation across the organisation. For example:
  - country codes;
  - currency codes;
  - units of measure (e.g. kilometres, kilograms, litres);
  - customer segments (e.g. retail, wholesale); and
  - product categories (e.g. clothing, electronics, furniture).
- **Transactional data**: Dynamic, ever-changing data generated by business activities, transactional data captures specific events or interactions and is typically used for operational purposes. For example:
  - sales orders and invoices;
  - customer service interactions;
  - inventory movements (e.g. stock in and stock out);
  - manufacturing production data; and
  - website clickstream data (e.g. user activity on a website).

Data architecture versus data design

Data architecture and data design are interrelated concepts that both play a crucial role in managing an organisation's data effectively, but they have distinct purposes and areas of focus:

- **Data architecture**: Refers to both a discipline and the resultant blueprints created through the application of that discipline. With regard to the latter, the data architecture is the high-level blueprint that defines how data is stored, managed, accessed and used throughout, and outside, an organisation. It encompasses the entire data ecosystem, including technologies, tools, processes, standards and security measures.

  Data architects make strategic decisions about how data will be integrated, shared and governed, considering factors such as data security, scalability, performance and compliance with regulations.

Typical examples of data architecture activities include:

- choosing a cloud storage platform;
- defining data security protocols;
- establishing data governance policies; and
- outlining strategies for data integration across different systems.

- **Data design**: Similarly to data architecture, data design can refer to both a discipline and the resultant artefacts. With regard to the latter, the data design is a set of detailed specifications that focus on the specific structure and organisation of data within a particular digital solution.

  Data designers translate the data architecture guidelines, standards and principles into concrete models that are relevant to a specific digital solution. They ensure that the data design will enable the realisation of the functional requirements for the solution while also incorporating mechanisms to maintain the accuracy and consistency of the data, and its efficient use for querying and analysis.

  Typical examples of data design activities include:

  - designing a schema for a customer database;
  - defining data types and constraints for different fields in a table; and
  - establishing naming conventions for data elements.

Taking the analogy of building a house, data architecture is like the overall blueprint that defines the foundation, layout, plumbing, electrical wiring and other essential aspects of the house, while data design is like specifying the exact dimensions of each room, the type of flooring materials and the placement of doors and windows.

In essence, data architecture provides the big picture and sets the course, while data design provides the detailed roadmap to follow. The relationship between architecture and design is explored further in Chapter 7.

Logical data design versus physical data design

The original idea of separating logical data design from physical database implementation can be traced back to the work of Peter Chen in the 1970s (Chen, 1976). This separation enables the logical design to be specified in more business or application terms, agnostic of the technology used to implement it. The logical design can then be adapted (a process referred to as 'tuning') to different technological implementations. This approach has remained valuable over time, accommodating the evolution of database technologies such as hierarchical, network, relational, object-oriented and graph databases. A single logical model can be translated into multiple physical designs (as discussed in Chapter 2), each tailored to different database technologies.

Developers of non-database solutions do not typically perform separate logical and physical data design activities. However, they do consider similar principles (such as logical data independence) when designing data structures and determining how data will be managed within the solution.

DATA DESIGN AND DOMAIN-DRIVEN DESIGN

Data design and domain-driven design (DDD) are closely interconnected, with the domain model in DDD (see Chapter 2) shaping the core concepts and relationships that directly influence data structures, ensuring consistency between the system's logic and underlying data.

DDD's bounded contexts segment data into manageable domains, reducing complexity and enabling tailored data models for each context. In event-driven DDD, domain events guide the design of data storage and its evolution over time. Collaboration between domain experts and developers in DDD further refines data design, ensuring it remains aligned with evolving business requirements.

Event storming is a technique that enables collaborative discovery of domain events, which form the basis for understanding workflows, identifying key data elements and designing event-driven systems aligned with the domain.

DATA DESIGN TECHNIQUES

The techniques use to design the data structures and formats to be used within a digital solution will depend on the particular use of the data and the technologies selected to support that use, for example whether designing data structures and formats for the persistent storage of the data (data at rest) or for the transmission of data between objects, components, services or even disparate applications, during runtime (data in transit). Additionally, whether designing for OLTP, OLAP solutions, smart and IoT devices, mobile apps or AI applications.

Comprehensive coverage of all the techniques currently in use is outside the scope of this book, so instead this chapter explores the most commonly used techniques.

Data design for OLTP solutions

Data design techniques for OLTP solutions prioritise efficiency, speed and data integrity for handling a high volume of concurrent transactions. The optimal data design depends on the specific characteristics of the solution, such as transaction volume, query patterns, data size and desired level of performance. It is often an iterative process, starting with a normalised model and then fine-tuning based on performance analysis.

Relational modelling and normalisation
Relational modelling and normalisation stemmed from the work of Edgar (Ted) F. Codd in the early 1970s. Widely considered to be the 'father of relational databases', in 1970, while working at the IBM San Jose Research Laboratory (now IBM Research – Almaden), Codd, a mathematician and computer scientist, published a ground-breaking paper entitled 'A relational model of data for large shared data banks' (Codd, 1970). This paper introduced the fundamental concepts of relational databases:

- **Tables (relations)**: Two-dimensional structures that store data in rows and columns.

- **Attributes (columns)**: The properties or characteristics of the data stored in each column.

- **Tuples (rows)**: Individual records within a table.

- **Keys**: Unique identifiers that enable efficient data retrieval and manipulation. Relationships between tables are established through foreign keys, which are columns in one table that reference the primary key (unique identifier) of another table. This ensures data consistency and integrity across the database.

- **Relational algebra**: A set of operations for manipulating data in relational databases.

- **Data normalisation**: Techniques to structure data efficiently and minimise redundancy.

Codd's work established a theoretical foundation for relational databases, which was supplemented in the mid-1970s with work by Chris Date, author of the seminal book *An Introduction to Database Systems* (Date, 2004), now in its eighth edition. Date was working at IBM's Systems Development Center in California at the time, where he was responsible for the design of a database language called Unified Database Language (UDL) and latterly the design of IBM's DB2 relational database. He played a crucial role in translating Codd's theoretical concepts into practical implementations, paving the way for the development of relational database management systems (RDBMSs) in the late 1970s and 1980s.

Normalisation (also referred to as relational data analysis or RDA) is a key data design technique used to derive a set of logical data structures that can be implemented using an RDBMS. Date provides comprehensive coverage of the normalisation process, which is beyond the scope of this book. However, Figure 5.5 provides an overview, which is briefly described below.

Figure 5.5 The normalisation process (© Assist Knowledge Development Ltd)

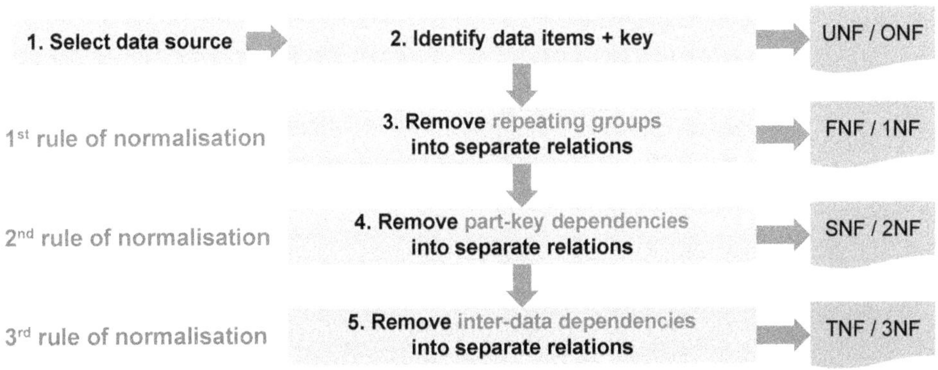

The normalisation process begins with a structured, but un-normalised, dataset (step 1 in Figure 5.5). The dataset may be obtained from a variety of sources such as:

- system inputs in the form of data entry forms or incoming message formats;
- system outputs in the form of reports or outgoing message formats; and
- legacy storage in various formats (including spreadsheets).

The un-normalised dataset is referred to as being in **un-normalised form**, which is denoted as 0NF or UNF. An extract from an un-normalised spreadsheet for a supplier of computing equipment and accessories is shown in Figure 5.6. The address values in this dataset have been shorted for display purposes and the ellipses (...) used to indicate that there is more detail that has been omitted.

Normalisation progresses through a sequence of refinements, each of which results in a further **normal form**. Each normal form is achieved by applying a normalisation rule. Figure 5.7 shows a normalisation worksheet that demonstrates the progressive normalisation of the dataset in Figure 5.6 from UNF through FNF/1NF (first normal form), SNF/2NF (second normal form) and TNF/3NF (third normal form). While there are additional normal forms (fourth normal form, fifth normal form and Boyce–Codd normal form), most data designers stop at TNF, and data structures that are in TNF are considered to be normalised.

In Figure 5.7, the UNF/0NF column comprises a list of attributes found in the source dataset, with the **primary key** (order no) underlined to distinguish it from non-key attributes. A primary key comprises one or more attributes that uniquely identify a given row in the dataset. When a primary key comprises a single attribute (as in this case), it is referred to as a **simple key**.

The attributes that are uniquely identified by a primary key are referred to as being dependent on the primary key. This concept of data dependency is fundamental to normalisation.

First normal form is derived by applying the first rule of normalisation to the UNF dataset. This rule states:

A relation is in first normal form if and only if all underlying domains contain atomic values only.

This rather academic definition can be translated into a much clearer instruction:

Remove repeating groups into separate relations.

The term **relation** is a key concept in relational theory, which refers to a two-dimensional data structure, or table. Essentially a relation is a collection of data attributes (the columns of the table), with the rows representing the individual data records. The fact

Figure 5.6 Un-normalised dataset

Order no	date	a/c no	customer name	delivery address	billing address	product code	description	unit price	quantity
784231	28-Jun	T2351	Will Knight	Unit 3 Avon Industrial Estate, ...	15a Acacia Gardens, ...	N570	WiFi 6E Mesh System	379.99	20
						N326	8 Port Gigabit Switch	24.99	30
						C744	2.5 Gigabit PCI Adapter	29.99	15
784232	28-Jun	R1782	Helen Smart	Flat 1, 76 West Street, ...	Flat 1, 76 West Street, ...	L451	15" Laptop, Intel i5 ...	369.99	1
						A212	15" Laptop Backpack	23.99	1
784233	28-Jun	R5429	Mosi Adebayo	22 The Avenue, ...	22 The Avenue, ...	A194	USB-C to Lightning cable	19.00	2
784234	28-Jun	R3376	Manjit Patel	Rose Cottage, New Street,...	Rose Cottage, New Street,...	C527	Wireless keyboard & mouse	33.99	1
...		...	...	...	...	...	...	...	...

81

Figure 5.7 Normalisation worksheet

UNF/0NF	FNF/1NF	SNF/2NF	TNF/3NF
order no date a/c no customer name delivery address billing address product code description unit price quantity	order no date a/c no customer name delivery address billing address *order no product code description unit price quantity	order no date a/c no customer name delivery address billing address *order no *product code quantity product code description unit price	order no date *a/c no delivery address *order no *product code quantity product code description unit price a/c no customer name billing address

that relations are two-dimensional is critical. This means that any given intersection of row and column should contain a single, atomic value. This is not true of the dataset in Figure 5.6, because the first row contains three values for product code, description, unit price and quantity. Similarly, row 2 contains two values for each of these attributes, so these attributes form a **repeating group**, and, following the instruction above, are removed to form a separate, new relation to create FNF/1NF, as shown in Figure 5.7.

The removal of the repeating group has also necessitated the creation of a new **foreign key** (order no) in the newly created relation, which is necessary to maintain the relationship with the original dataset, which now contains fewer attributes following the removal of product code, description, unit price and quantity. The new foreign key corresponds to the primary key of the related dataset (order no), which is copied into the new relation, where it is referred to as a foreign key. In Figure 5.7, foreign keys have been denoted using an asterisk (*) before the name of the attribute.

The new foreign key also forms part of the primary key of the new relation because, in order to uniquely identify a given combination of the attributes description, unit price and quantity, it is necessary to know both the order no and product code values. Consequently, in the new relation, order no is said to be a **prime-foreign key**, denoted by the combination of underline and asterisk.

Second normal form is derived by applying the second rule of normalisation to the 1NF dataset. This rule states:

> A relation is in second normal form (2NF) if and only if it is in 1NF and every non-key attribute is fully dependent on the primary key.

This definition emphasises the progressive nature of normalisation, as a prerequisite for each normal form is that the dataset is at least in the previous normal form. Again, this definition is somewhat confusing, so it is easier to understand when translated into the instruction:

Remove part-key dependencies into separate relations.

A part-key dependency occurs when the primary key of a relation is made up of two or more data items (referred to as a **concatenated key**), and one or more of the non-key attributes is only dependent on part of the key rather than all of it. For example, in the new relation created in 1NF, the values of the attributes description and unit price can be uniquely determined by knowing the value of the product code alone; the order no attribute is not relevant. Consequently, the description and unit price attributes are part-key dependencies and are removed from the second relation of 1NF to form a new, third relation in the SNF/2NF column of the normalisation worksheet. The primary key of the new relation is therefore product code, which makes the product code attribute in the second relation a foreign key, or more correctly, a prime-foreign key. Where each element of a concatenated key also acts as a foreign key, it is referred to as a **compound key**. Hence, the key of the second relation in the SNF/2NF column of the normalisation worksheet is a compound key.

Third normal form is derived by applying the third rule of normalisation to the 2NF dataset. This rule states:

A relation is in third normal form (3NF) if and only if it is in 2NF and every non-key attribute is non-transitively dependent on the primary key.

Again, this rather complex definition is easier to understand when translated into the instruction:

Remove inter-data dependencies into separate relations.

An inter-data dependency occurs when a non-key attribute is indirectly (transitively) dependent on the primary key of the relation, but directly dependent on another non-key attribute. For example, in the first relation in 2NF, the values of the attributes customer name and billing address, despite being dependent on the primary key of the relation (there will only be one corresponding value of customer name and billing address for a given order), are uniquely determined by the customer's a/c no. In other words, for a specific value of the a/c no attribute (such as R5429), the corresponding values can be determined for customer name (Mosi Adebayo) and billing address (22 The Avenue, ...). Consequently, the customer name and billing address attributes are inter-data (transitive) dependencies and are removed from the first relation of 2NF to form a new, fourth relation in the TNF/3NF column of the normalisation worksheet, with the primary key a/c no.

Normalisation can be used to develop a set of data tables for a digital solution from the prototype inputs and outputs developed during I/O design, as well as from a range of documents used in the business processes to be supported by the new solution. These tables form the logical data design and can be 'tuned' to produce a physical data design, discussed later in this chapter.

In practice, a number of data sources will each be individually normalised and the resultant sets of relations rationalised into a single set of **rationalised relations**. The rationalised relations can then be used to draw a special kind of data model known as a **TNF data model** (or just TNF model). This model (discussed below) can then be combined with the conceptual data model produced by the BA during system definition (the analysis data model) to arrive at the final logical data design.

A further issue that the designer may encounter is that the analysis data model is incomplete. Additional data items (attributes), and even additional classes (tables) are often required to support certain processing defined during the process design stage, or to enable future system flexibility in the form of configuration parameters.

TNF data models
TNF data models use ERD notation as this is a de facto standard for data designers and database administrators. However, these are not to be confused with analysis data models that use ERD notation, as TNF models do not show optionality, exclusivity or relationship names – these constructs are determined when conducting business discussions to derive a top-down logical data model during solution definition.

Figure 5.8 shows a TNF model based on the TNF relations in Figure 5.7.

The crows foot symbol (⅄) in Figure 5.8 denotes 'many' and the absence of the crows foot denotes 'one', because normalisation automatically resolves 'many-to-many' relationships so that the resultant data structures comprise just 'one-to-many' relationships. For example, one Customer can be related to many Orders but each Order can only be related to one Customer.

While the TNF model provides a visual representation of a logical data structure that identifies the attributes contained in each table/relation/entity/class, the detailed definition of these attributes is typically recorded as part of a **data dictionary**. Figure 5.9 shows an example of an **attribute description** for the a/c no attribute, which would typically form part of a data dictionary.

Physical data design for OLTP solutions
Physical data design involves 'tuning' the logical design to produce a technology-specific implementation. The most obvious choice of technology to use for a normalised logical data design is a relational database, managed through an RDBMS. Microsoft Azure SQL, Amazon Relational Database Service and Oracle Autonomous Database are popular choices for cloud-based, hosted RDBMS solutions.

The physical data design process for translating a normalised logical data design into an RDBMS schema involves the following activities:

- Each TNF relation in the logical data model becomes a table in the RDBMS schema, with a column for each attribute within the relation. Figure 5.10 shows the resultant tables based on the TNF model in Figure 5.8.

Figure 5.8 TNF data model

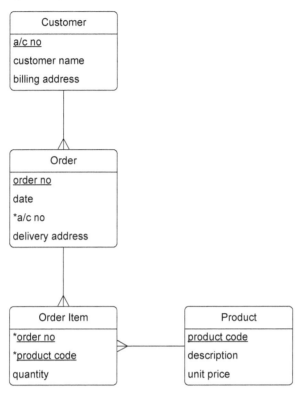

- A data type (e.g. text, number (including integer and real number formats), date, Boolean (yes/no values)) is specified for each column of each table.

- Each table in the RDBMS schema is indexed by its primary key. Indexes enable direct access to the data using a value of the key.

- Where the primary key of a table is a compound key, an index is created for each attribute of the compound key.

- Indexes are defined for each foreign key and each non-key access requirement. In this context indexes enable faster navigation through the data records in a table to extract those required, rather than having to search through the entire table.

The designer also needs to take account of factors such as storage capacity and performance requirements, and how best to use the features offered by the particular DBMS to minimise the following:

- data access time;

- processing time;

- application development time;

- database maintenance time;

Figure 5.9 Attribute description for a/c no attribute

Attribute name	a/c no
Synonyms	Customer number
Description	A unique account number assigned to an individual or entity for identification
Source	Automatically generated by finance system when a new customer account is created
Data format	A9999
Data type	Alphanumeric (1 alphabetic character followed by 4 numeric characters)
Example values	T1234, R5678
Validation rules	- Must match the format A9999. - The first character must be a single uppercase letter. Permitted values are T (for trade customers) and R (for retail customers). - The next four characters must be numeric digits (0–9).
Optionality	Mandatory
Remarks	Used as a unique identifier for customer accounts

- use of persistent storage;
- the need for database reorganisation; and
- process and UI complexity.

The logical data structures themselves may also be fine-tuned based on performance analysis. This fine-tuning is often referred to as **denormalisation** and can involve undoing some of the interventions made during the normalisation process, such as:

- Introducing redundant or derived data in the form of counts or totals, or duplicating data in more than one table to reduce the access path or the number of accesses for a particular transaction (see data navigation diagrams below).

- Combining logically separate tables to reduce the number of database accesses for a particular transaction. This essentially reintroduces inter-data dependencies.

- Splitting a single table so that a smaller volume of data is transferred during a transaction. Splitting can either be done vertically (by moving a subset of non-key attributes into a separate table with the same key as the original table), or horizontally (by removing a subset of rows to a separate table, with an identical structure to the original table). The latter is essentially what happens when historical data is archived.

Figure 5.10 Tables derived from the TNF data model in Figure 5.8

Customer

a/c no	customer name	billing address
R1782	Helen Smart	Flat 1, 76 West Street, ...
R3376	Manjit Patel	Rose Cottage, New Street,...
R5429	Mosi Adebayo	22 The Avenue, ...
T2351	Will Knight	15a Acacia Gardens, ...
...	...	...

Order

Order no	date	a/c no	delivery address
784231	28-Jun	T2351	Unit 3 Avon Industrial Estate, ...
784232	28-Jun	R1782	Flat 1, 76 West Street, ...
784233	28-Jun	R5429	22 The Avenue, ...
784234	28-Jun	R3376	Rose Cottage, New Street,...
...	...	...	...

Order Item

Order no	product code	quantity
784231	N570	20
784231	N326	30
784231	C744	15
784232	L451	1
784232	A212	1
784233	A194	2
784234	C527	1
...	...	...

Product

product code	description	unit price
A194	USB-C to Lightning cable	19.00
A212	15" Laptop Backpack	23.99
C527	Wireless keyboard & mouse	33.99
C744	2.5 Gigabit PCI Adapter	29.99
L451	15" Laptop, Intel i5 ...	369.99
N326	8 Port Gigabit Switch	24.99
N570	WiFi 6E Mesh System	379.99
...	...	...

Denormalisation is a trade-off between (1) data access and processing times and (2) application development time and process complexity, as it is more complex to access multiple tables than the case where all of the data resides in a single table.

Data navigation diagrams

Part of the physical data design process described above involves fine-tuning the physical data structures (denormalisation) based on performance analysis, and potentially introducing additional indexes to minimise data access times. This activity is aided significantly when the designer understands how the data needs to be accessed (access paths) to support specific requirements.

In the mid-1980s, James Martin popularised a diagramming technique known as a data navigation diagram (DND), which enabled system analysts and designers to visualise how to navigate through a database (Martin and McClure, 1985). The original notation has since evolved, and Figure 5.11 provides an example that uses a more recent incarnation of the notation.

Figure 5.11 Data navigation diagram

DNDs were originally developed from ERDs, but can equally be devised from class diagrams or any other logical model of a data structure. The example in Figure 5.11 is based on the TNF model in Figure 5.8 and shows an access path through the data structure to fulfil the following requirement:

> List all orders and their customers for a specified product code, to include the attributes: product code, description, order no, quantity, date, a/c no and customer name.

The use of a single arrowhead denotes that a single row (record) will be accessed. For example, based on the primary key of the `Product` relation (`product code`), which is an input for the first data access, there will be a single row of the `Product` table/relation retrieved. The double arrowhead represents that, for a given row of the `Product` table retrieved, there can be multiple (one or more) corresponding rows of `Order Item` retrieved. Then, for each `Order Item` row retrieved, there will be a single `Order` row retrieved, and for that `Order`, a single `Customer` row will be retrieved.

As a consequence of TNF models not showing the optionality of relationships, the DND in Figure 5.11 assumes that all data accesses are mandatory (denoted by the solid line).

The class diagram in Figure 5.12 shows optionality, which can also be represented explicitly on the DND (see Figure 5.13).

The DND in Figure 5.13 provides a more complete view, as it shows the optional access (denoted by the dashed line) of `Order Item`, as, according to the class diagram in Figure 5.12, not all `Product` rows will be associated with `Order Items`. It also shows the attributes being retrieved from each class/table.

Data design for OLAP solutions

Data design techniques for OLAP solutions differ from those used for OLTP solutions due to the focus on complex data analysis and retrieval of aggregated datasets, rather than high volumes of transactions. While there are multiple diverse technologies in this space, which overlaps with the world of big data, one design technique that dominates is dimensional modelling.

Figure 5.12 Class diagram showing optionality

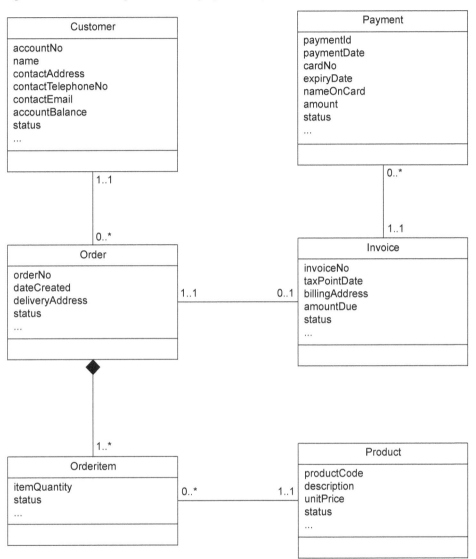

Dimensional modelling

Dimensional modelling is a data design technique developed by Ralph Kimball. The approach described by Kimball and Ross (2013) has become the most widely accepted method for structuring information in data warehouse and business intelligence (BI) solutions.

Fundamental to dimensional modelling are **facts** and **dimensions**. Facts are essentially measurements (which is why they are also referred to as **measures**) that are captured by an organisation's business processes and their supporting information systems, for

Figure 5.13 Data navigation diagram showing optional data access

example the value of an order or the mark achieved in an examination. Kimball and Ross explain that:

> facts are surrounded by largely textual context that is true at the moment the fact is recorded. This context is intuitively divided into independent logical clumps called dimensions, [which] describe the 'who, what, when, where, why and how' context of the measurement.

For example, in the case of the 'value of an order' fact (named `order amount` from hereon for ease of reference), a dimension could represent the date and time the order was taken, or the customer who placed the order. Similarly, in the case of the `examination mark` fact, a dimension could be `examination subject` or `examination centre`.

Combining facts and dimensions enables information to be aggregated (totalled, averaged, counted and so on) in different ways, for example to derive the total value of orders (sum of `order amount` fact) for a given day, month, quarter or year, or for a given customer, or to derive the average `examination mark` for a particular `examination subject` or `examination centre`.

Potentially, each business area or business process within an organisation can be represented by its own dimensional model that comprises a **fact table** containing the various measurements relevant to that area or process (measures), surrounded by a series of **dimension tables** containing the contextual details.

The **grain** of a fact table defines the level of detail or granularity of the data stored. It determines what a single record in the fact table represents, for example a single transaction, a daily summary or a monthly total. Choosing the right grain is crucial because it impacts the size of the fact table and the performance of any queries devised to access the data.

Fact and dimension tables are organised into **star schemas**, and a popular variant is called a **snowflake schema**.

Star schemas
A star schema is a type of database schema used in data warehouse and BI solutions that is designed to optimise the organisation, storage and retrieval of data for analytical purposes. It is one of the simplest and most widely used schema designs, characterised by its straightforward and intuitive structure, that resembles the shape of a star.

Figure 5.14 shows a star schema for a sales order processing business function.

Figure 5.14 Star schema for a sales order processing business function

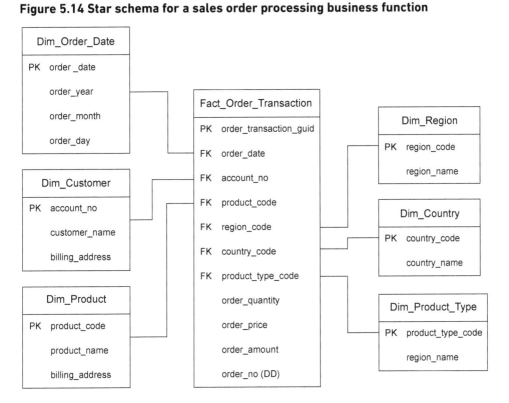

At the heart of a star schema is a large central table known as the **fact table**. This table stores quantitative data or metrics, such as the order_quantity, order_price and order_amount attributes in Figure 5.14, in addition to foreign keys (denoted by the FK prefix to the appropriate attribute name) that link to **dimension tables**. The dimension tables store descriptive attributes related to the facts, providing context for the data in the fact table. The PK prefix denotes the primary key for each table, which in the dimension tables corresponds to the relevant foreign key in the fact table. The fact table uses a **surrogate key** (order-transaction_guid) for the primary key. Note that the order_no attribute is suffixed with (DD). This denotes this attribute as a **degenerate dimension**, which is an attribute that is used as a dimension but where there is no associated dimension table, because the only meaningful attribute for the dimension is the key itself.

Snowflake schemas
A snowflake schema is an extension of the star schema described above. It is designed to handle complex data relationships by normalising dimension tables into multiple related tables. This results in a more intricate structure that resembles a snowflake, hence the name.

Figure 5.15 shows a snowflake schema equivalent of the star schema in Figure 5.14.

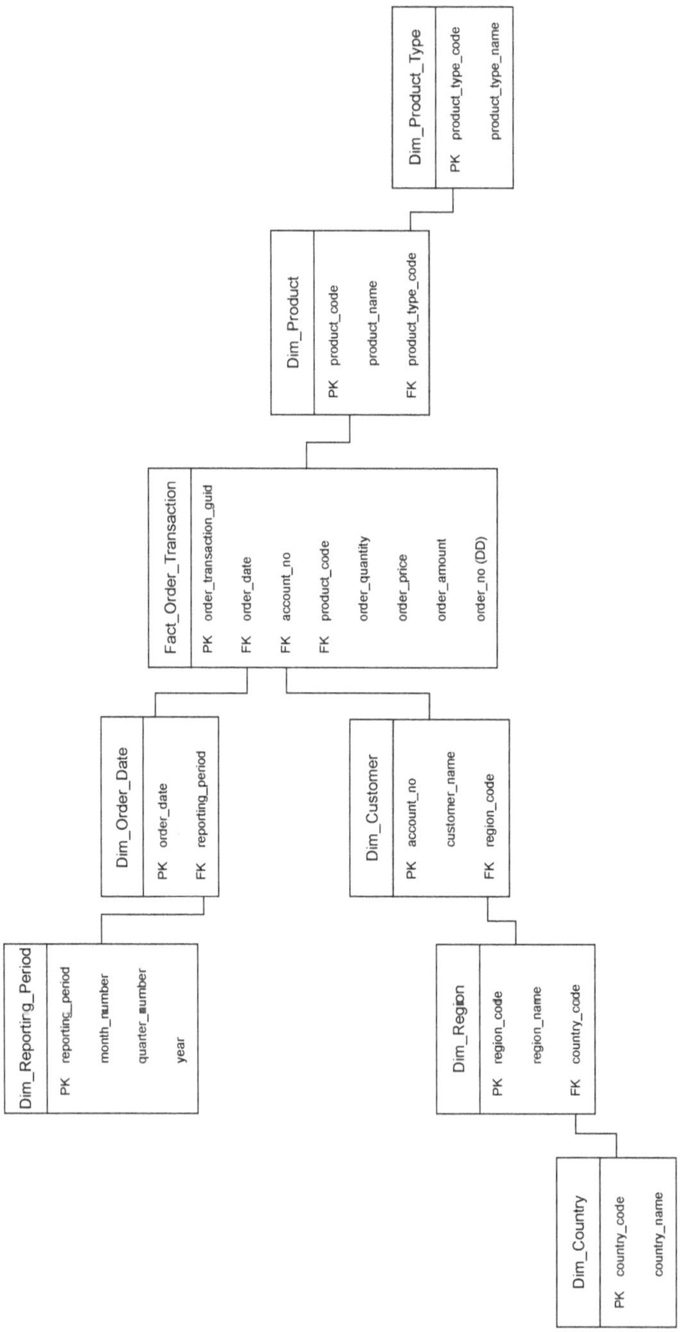

Figure 5.15 Snowflake schema for a sales order processing business function

Dim_Reporting_Period	
PK	reporting_period
	month_number
	quarter_number
	year

Dim_Order_Date	
PK	order_date
FK	reporting_period

Fact_Order_Transaction	
PK	order_transaction_guid
FK	order_date
FK	account_no
FK	product_code
	order_quantity
	order_price
	order_amount
	order_no (DD)

Dim_Customer	
PK	account_no
	customer_name
FK	region_code

Dim_Region	
PK	region_code
	region_name
FK	country_code

Dim_Country	
PK	country_code
	country_name

Dim_Product	
PK	product_code
	product_name
FK	product_type_code

Dim_Product_Type	
PK	product_type_code
	product_type_name

Star schema and snowflake schema comparison

While star schemas and snowflake schemas both support OLAP solutions, choosing between them is often a challenge for the solution designer. Table 5.2 summarises the key differences between the two and typical uses for each schema type.

Table 5.2 Star and snowflake schema comparison

Aspect	Star schema	Snowflake schema
Structure	• Simple design resembling a star, comprising a central fact table connected to multiple dimension tables. • Dimension tables are usually denormalised – they contain all relevant attributes in a single table.	• More complex design resembling a snowflake pattern, comprising a central fact table connected to multiple dimension tables. • Dimension tables are normalised – split into multiple related tables, where dimensions are organised in a hierarchical manner.
Data redundancy	• Denormalisation in dimension tables leads to some data redundancy, where the same data might be repeated across multiple rows in a table. • Data redundancy simplifies query execution and reduces the number of table joins required.	• Normalisation reduces redundancy by storing each piece of data only once. • The reduction in redundancy requires more tables and potentially more complex joins, increasing the complexity of managing and querying the data.
Query performance	• As a consequence of denormalised dimension tables, fewer joins are needed in queries, leading to faster performance, especially in read-heavy operations typical of data warehousing.	• More joins are required due to the normalised structure, which can slow down query performance.
Storage efficiency	• Denormalisation typically requires more storage space as the same data may be duplicated across the dimension tables. • The increased storage requirement is a trade-off for faster query performance.	• Normalisation reduces data duplication, resulting in more efficient use of storage space. • The focus on minimising storage comes at the cost of potentially slower query performance.

(Continued)

Table 5.2 (Continued)

Aspect	Star schema	Snowflake schema
Ease of use	• The simple and flat structure is easier for business users to understand and use. • Writing queries is more straightforward, as there are fewer tables to join. • Non-technical users, such as BAs, often find the star schema easier to work with.	• The hierarchical and normalised structure can be more challenging for users to understand and work with. • Writing queries in a snowflake schema can be more complicated due to the need for multiple joins across related tables.
Maintenance and scalability	• With fewer tables and simpler relationships, the star schema is generally easier to maintain and scale as data grows. • The schema can handle large volumes of data and is straightforward to expand by adding new dimensions or facts.	• The added complexity of managing multiple related tables can make maintenance more challenging. • While scalable, the complexity of the schema can make it more difficult to manage as data and relationships grow.
Common uses	Star schemas are particularly effective for ad hoc queries, dashboards and reporting systems where simplicity and speed are important.	Snowflake schemas are better suited for situations where: • data relationships are intricate and require more complex queries that necessitate navigating hierarchical data structures; • storage efficiency and data integrity are more important than query speed.

Physical data design for OLAP solutions

The physical implementation of a dimensional model involves creating fact and dimension tables in a database system such as a data warehouse, where they are implemented as multidimensional cubes. Effective physical implementation also considers factors such as granularity, indexing, partitioning and aggregation to ensure the data warehouse performs efficiently and scales with the data.

As well as using dedicated data warehouse technologies, star and snowflake schemas can be mapped directly to tables within a relational database for deployment. An example of the SQL statements used to create a sales fact table and a time dimension table are shown in Figure 5.16.

Figure 5.16 Sample SQL statements used to create fact and dimension tables

```
CREATE TABLE FactSales (
    Sales_ID INT PRIMARY KEY,
    Time_ID INT,
    Product_ID INT,
    Customer_ID INT,
    Sales_Amount DECIMAL(10,2),
    Units_Sold INT,
    FOREIGN KEY (Time_ID) REFERENCES DimTime(Time_ID),
    FOREIGN KEY (Product_ID) REFERENCES DimProduct(Product_ID),
    FOREIGN KEY (Customer_ID) REFERENCES DimCustomer(Customer_ID)
);

CREATE TABLE DimTime (
    Time_ID INT PRIMARY KEY,
    Year INT,
    Quarter INT,
    Month INT,
    Day INT,
    DayOfWeek VARCHAR(10)
);
```

A brief review of data technologies is provided later in this chapter.

Data design for microservices

A core principle of microservices is that each service owns and manages its own data. This promotes autonomy and faster development cycles for individual services. Consequently, a common approach to data design for microservices is for each microservice to have its own private database. This database may use local or cloud-based relational or Not Only SQL (NoSQL) database technology, or it may even use proprietary data file formats (see popular data technologies later in this chapter), depending on what data is relevant to that service's functionality. Microservice data ownership simplifies deployment, scaling and data security management for each service.

Where the private database option is not practical, due to the desire to share a common database across an organisation, the use of data views can emulate the concept by exposing only the data from the shared database that is relevant to the service, keeping all other data hidden.

In his book *Monolith to Microservices: Evolutionary Patterns to Transform Your Monolith* (Newman, 2020), Sam Newman provides a set of patterns for dealing with legacy databases when moving to a microservices architecture, and one particularly useful pattern he presents for using shared databases when building a microservices architecture is the '**database wrapping service**'. As Newman explains:

Sometimes, when something is too hard to deal with, hiding the mess can make sense. With the database wrapping service, we do exactly that: hide the database behind a service that acts as a thin wrapper, moving database dependencies to become service dependencies.

The database wrapping service pattern is demonstrated in Figure 5.17.

Figure 5.17 Using a service to wrap a database

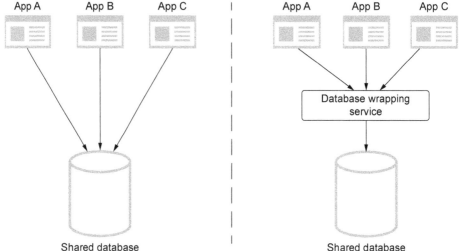

The database wrapping service can be used with any digital solution, especially where the solution is accessing legacy databases or databases based on legacy technology, but it works particularly well with a microservices architecture because microservices communicate with each other through APIs, which can be used to retrieve or update data required by other services, following a request–response pattern. These APIs expose the business capabilities of the service, hiding the underlying data storage details from the service consumer.

Data consistency

Several approaches can be used to ensure data consistency between microservices, including:

- **Event sourcing**: Storing a sequence of events that led to the current data state enables the replaying of events to achieve consistency across services.

- **API choreography**: Services coordinate data updates through a series of well-defined API calls, ensuring a consistent sequence of operations.

- **Saga pattern**: Manages long-running transactions that involve multiple services. If a failure occurs, the saga pattern can roll back changes across all involved services.

Data serialisation

Data serialisation is essentially the process of converting complex data structures into a format that's easier to store or transmit, enabling different programs/services/systems, potentially written in different languages, to exchange information. The designer must choose a suitable format, such as JSON or protocol buffers, for exchanging data between services efficiently.

Denormalisation

Denormalisation was introduced earlier in this chapter. In the context of microservices this may involve the application of techniques to optimise query performance within a microservice's database, and improve data access times, especially for frequently accessed data.

Trade-offs are common in data design, and, in the context of microservices the key trade-offs are between data ownership, consistency and manageability.

Data design for mobile apps and smart devices

Data design for smart devices goes hand in hand with data design for mobile apps. The data collected by smart devices needs to be structured and organised in a way that can be easily transmitted to and processed by the corresponding app.

There are three main areas to consider when undertaking data design for smart devices and mobile apps:

- the aspects that relate to the device itself;
- the data structures required by the app; and
- data transmission.

On the device itself

The designer needs to consider what data is being captured by sensors on the device and, to prevent overloading the device, identify the most critical data points captured that are required to support the app's functionality.

The data format to be used for efficient data transmission is another critical consideration. Popular options include JSON, protocol buffers or even custom-designed formats optimised for the specific data types involved.

The designer may also consider the use of preprocessing techniques on the device itself. This may involve filtering out noise, performing basic calculations or data compression to reduce the amount of data to be transmitted.

On the app

Just like any other digital solution, apps need a data schema to structure the data needed to support the features of the app, and provide persistent data storage. The data storage solution chosen by the designer needs to take account of data volumes, complexity and access patterns. Options include on-device storage, cloud databases or a hybrid approach.

Although internet connectivity has vastly improved in recent years, unfortunately it is not yet ubiquitous. Therefore, the designer must consider how the app will function when an internet connection is unavailable. This could involve caching data locally for offline access or implementing functionality that doesn't require a constant connection.

Data transmission considerations

As a large proportion of smart devices are battery-powered, optimising data transmission becomes important to conserve battery life. This might involve techniques like batching data or adjusting transmission frequency.

Another critical consideration concerning data transmission is the implementation of secure communication protocols to encrypt data during transmission between the device and the app, to protect sensitive information from unauthorised access. This aspect of design (along with user privacy and data security) is considered further in Chapter 6.

Additional considerations

Depending on the nature of the device and app, the designer may also need to consider scalability, as the number of devices and users grow. This might involve using cloud-based solutions or flexible data models.

Data design for the Internet of Things

The core principles of data design for smart devices and their apps and the IoT are similar. Both involve structuring and managing data from connected devices and the need for efficient storage, retrieval and analysis of data. Similarly, both need to consider scalability as the number of devices grows, and security and privacy are critical design considerations.

However, the specific considerations might differ based on the volume, complexity and purpose of the data collected. The most significant differences are explored below.

- **Data volume and velocity**: IoT devices often generate a higher volume and faster stream of data (e.g. readings from sensors such as thermostats) compared to some smart devices. This can impact storage and processing needs (see also *Big data* earlier in this chapter).

- **Data complexity**: Smart devices might involve more complex data structures if they have advanced features or use AI, for example a smart speaker might process not just voice commands but also contextual information.

- **Focus**: IoT data design often prioritises collecting and transmitting data efficiently, while the data design for a smart device might put more emphasis on local processing and analysis for real-time decision-making.

Data design for AI applications

AI is an evolving specialist area within computer science, and as such, providing detailed coverage of AI technologies and design methodologies would quickly become obsolete. The application of AI is also becoming more diverse every day. However, as with any digital solution, AI applications are only as effective as the data that underpin them (in the case of AI, the models such as LLMs). Well-designed data is essential for feeding AI models with the information they need to learn effectively, respond to requests and make decisions.

CONCURRENCY ISSUES IN DATA DESIGN

Concurrency issues arise when multiple users or processes access and manipulate data in a digital solution at the same time. These issues can lead to inconsistent, corrupted or incorrect data if not properly managed. Concurrency is particularly challenging in environments where data is frequently created and updated, such as databases in multi-user applications.

Concurrency issues are a major concern for the data designer and they manifest themselves in various ways. The following examples describe the behaviour of **transactions** – a sequence of one or more SQL operations, such as insert, update, delete, that are treated as a single logical database activity. The examples cited refer to rows in a dataset (table):

- **Lost updates**: These occur when two or more transactions simultaneously update the same data, and one update is overwritten or lost. For example: *Two users retrieve the same customer record to update it. The first user changes the address and saves it. The second user, who retrieved the old address, also saves their changes. The first user's update is lost.*

- **Dirty reads**: These occur when a transaction reads data that has been modified by another transaction but not yet committed. If the other transaction is rolled back (the changes are undone), the first transaction has read invalid data.

- **Non-repeatable reads**: These occur when a transaction reads the same row twice and gets different data each time because another transaction has modified the row in the meantime. For example: *In an application for booking seats on a flight, transaction A reads a row corresponding to a particular seat, which is available at the time, but just before confirming the booking the same transaction reads the same row again, but this time the seat is showing as taken, because transaction B has booked it in the meantime.*

- **Phantom reads**: These occur when a transaction reads a set of rows that satisfy a condition, but another transaction subsequently inserts or deletes rows that satisfy the same condition, causing the first transaction to see a different set of rows in subsequent reads. For example: *Transaction A reads all orders for a specified customer. Transaction B subsequently inserts a new order for the same customer. If transaction A re-executes the query, it sees a new row that wasn't there before.*

- **Write skew**: These occur when two transactions update different rows but those rows together violate a constraint when considered collectively. For example: *Two bank tellers simultaneously transfer money between two accounts. Each transaction checks the overall balance and finds it valid, but after both transactions commit, the overall balance is wrong.*

To manage these issues, various techniques can be employed, including:

- **Locking mechanisms**: There are two approaches when locking data:

  - **Pessimistic locking**: Transactions lock the data they access to prevent other transactions from accessing it until the lock is released. This can lead to deadlocks, where two or more transactions are waiting for each other's locks to be released, but it prevents concurrency issues effectively.

  - **Optimistic locking**: Transactions proceed without locking data, but before committing they check whether any other transaction has modified the data. If another modification has occurred, the transaction is rolled back.

- **Isolation levels**: An isolation level is a concept used in DBMS' to define how transaction integrity is maintained while multiple transactions are executed concurrently. When multiple transactions are running at the same time, they might access and modify the same data, leading to the issues identified above. Isolation levels determine the degree to which the operations in one transaction are isolated from the operations in other concurrent transactions.

- **Versioning**: In some database systems, multi-version concurrency control (MVCC) is used, where each transaction sees a snapshot of the database at a certain point in time. New versions of rows are created for each transaction, and conflicts are resolved by the database system.

- **Transaction management**: Transaction management in database systems is the process of ensuring that database transactions are processed reliably and adhere to the ACID properties: **atomic** (all or nothing), **consistent** (leave the database in a valid state), **isolated** (transactions do not affect each other), **durable** (once committed, changes are permanent). This typically involves the use of a two-phase commit protocol, which ensures that all nodes in a distributed database system either commit or roll back a transaction, avoiding partial commits that could lead to inconsistency.

- **Application-level strategies**: There are two commonly used strategies:

  - **Retry logic**: Implements logic to retry transactions that fail due to concurrency conflicts, especially in optimistic locking scenarios.

  - **Eventual consistency**: In distributed systems, sometimes strong consistency is sacrificed for availability and partition tolerance, with the understanding that the system will eventually become consistent.

Each method has its trade-offs between consistency, performance and complexity, and the choice of method often depends on the specific requirements of the solution being designed.

POPULAR DATA TECHNOLOGIES

Digital solution designers rely on a diverse array of tools and platforms to store, process, analyse and visualise data. From relational databases like Microsoft SQL Server, Oracle Database, IBM DB2, MySQL and PostgreSQL to cutting-edge big data frameworks like Apache Spark and Hadoop, the ecosystem of data technologies continues to evolve at a rapid pace. Cloud platforms such as Amazon Web Services (AWS), Google Cloud and Microsoft Azure have further revolutionised how data is managed, enabling scalability and flexibility like never before. Equally important are advancements in data science, ML frameworks and visualisation tools such as TensorFlow, Tableau and Power BI, which empower users to extract actionable insights.

This section explores the most popular data technologies as at the time of writing (January 2025), with examples and typical use cases.

Data storage technologies

Data storage technologies encompass systems and solutions designed to store, manage and access data efficiently. These technologies support various data types (structured, semi-structured and unstructured) and workloads, ranging from small-scale applications to vast big data environments. Table 5.3 summarises five popular categories of data storage technology, with examples and typical use cases, which are described further below.

Table 5.3 Summary of popular data storage technologies

Type	Examples	Use cases
Relational database	MySQL, PostgreSQL, Oracle Database, Microsoft SQL Server, IBM DB2	Ecommerce platforms, financial systems, ERP and CRM systems
NoSQL database	MongoDB, Redis, Cassandra, Neo4j (graph database)	Content management systems (MongoDB), social networks (Neo4j), real-time applications (Redis)
Data warehouse	Snowflake, Amazon Redshift, Google BigQuery	Business intelligence, marketing analytics, healthcare reporting
Data lake	Amazon S3, Azure Data Lake Storage, Hadoop Distributed File System (HDFS)	ML models, IoT data, advanced analytics (AWS S3)
Data lakehouse	Databricks Lakehouse Platform, Delta Lake, Apache Iceberg	Unified analytics (combining real-time and historical data analysis in a single platform), AI and ML pipelines, enterprise data management

Relational databases
Relational databases are structured data storage systems that organise information into tables with rows and columns, following a predefined schema. They use SQL for querying, updating and managing data, and are designed to handle complex relationships between data entities. Known for their reliability and data integrity, relational databases support ACID transactions, ensuring secure and consistent data retention.

Relational databases are widely used in applications requiring structured data and complex queries, such as ecommerce platforms, financial systems and ERP solutions.

NoSQL databases
NoSQL databases are a class of non-relational databases designed for flexibility, scalability and handling large volumes of unstructured, semi-structured or structured data. Unlike relational databases, they do not rely on fixed schemas and support diverse

101

data models, including document-based (e.g. MongoDB), key–value (e.g. Redis), column–family (e.g. Cassandra) and graph-based (e.g. Neo4j). NoSQL databases are optimised for distributed architectures, making them highly scalable and fault-tolerant. They excel in use cases such as real-time analytics, content management, IoT data storage and social networks, where traditional relational databases may struggle to handle the dynamic and voluminous nature of data.

Data warehouses

Data warehouses are specialised systems designed to consolidate and analyse large volumes of data from various sources, for reporting and decision-making. They are optimised for read-heavy operations, complex queries and OLAP workloads, enabling organisations to derive insights from historical and aggregated data. Modern data warehouses offer cloud-based scalability, high performance and integration with analytics tools. They support structured and semi-structured data, making them ideal for business intelligence, trend analysis, customer behaviour insights and enterprise-wide analytics. These technologies enable organisations to make data-driven decisions by providing a centralised, efficient platform for querying and visualising data.

Data lakes

Data lakes accommodate large volumes of raw (unprocessed), unstructured, semi-structured and structured data in their original formats, offering exceptional flexibility and scalability. Unlike data warehouses, data lakes do not require a predefined schema when data is ingested, allowing seamless integration of diverse data types from various sources. They provide cost-effective storage solutions and are designed to integrate with big data processing frameworks. Ideal for data science, ML and advanced analytics, data lakes enable organisations to store and analyse extensive datasets without relying on predefined data models, making them a good choice for managing complex, high-volume data environments.

Data lakehouses

Data lakehouses combine the best features of data lakes and data warehouses into a unified architecture, offering the scalability and flexibility of data lakes with the performance and structure of data warehouses. They enable the storage of raw, unstructured, semi-structured and structured data while supporting schema enforcement, ACID transactions and high-performance analytics. Data lakehouse technologies provide seamless integration with big data frameworks and ML tools, enabling organisations to run advanced analytics and real-time queries on large datasets. Data lakehouses eliminate the need for separate data silos, making them ideal for enterprises seeking cost-efficient, versatile solutions for business intelligence, data science and ML workloads.

Data serialisation technologies

Data serialisation technologies are used to convert data structures or objects into a format that can be easily transmitted and reconstructed. They are essential for data exchange between systems, especially in distributed applications. Serialisation ensures compatibility, reduces data size and facilitates efficient communication. Common formats differ in structure, performance and readability, catering to various use cases.

Table 5.4 provides an overview of popular data serialisation technologies (with typical use cases), which are described below.

Table 5.4 Summary of popular data serialisation technologies

Technology	Use cases
JSON	Lightweight data exchange, RESTful APIs
XML	Configuration files, legacy systems, SOAP APIs
Protobuf	High-performance applications, gRPC communication
Avro	Apache Hadoop and big data ecosystems
MessagePack	Performance-critical applications requiring small datasets
YAML	Configuration files, development operations (DevOps) tools such as Kubernetes

JSON

JavaScript Object Notation (JSON) is a lightweight, text-based data serialisation format that is easy to read and write for humans and straightforward to analyse for machines. It represents data as key–value pairs and supports hierarchical structures such as objects, arrays (structured collections of elements, typically of the same data type) and nested data, making it versatile for a variety of applications. Widely used in web development, APIs and configuration files due to its compatibility with most programming languages and frameworks, JSON's simplicity and flexibility make it ideal for lightweight data exchange, although it may be less efficient than binary formats such as Protobuf or Avro in performance-critical scenarios.

XML

eXtensible Markup Language (XML) is a flexible, text-based data serialisation format designed to store and transport structured data in a self-descriptive manner. It uses a hierarchical, tag-based syntax that allows for complex data representation and supports attributes and nested elements (where an element is contained within another of the same or a related type). XML is highly extensible and supports schema validation, enabling strict data structure definitions. While it is human-readable, its verbose syntax often results in larger file sizes compared to alternatives such as JSON or binary formats. XML is widely used in legacy systems, document storage and SOAP-based web services, making it a good choice for applications requiring rich data description and cross-platform compatibility.

Protobuf

Protocol buffers (Protobuf) is a highly efficient, compact and schema-based data serialisation technology developed by Google. It uses a binary format that significantly reduces data size and improves processing speed compared to text-based formats such as JSON and XML. Protobuf requires a defined schema using `.proto` files, which outline the structure and types of the data, enabling strong typing (a programming language characteristic where variables are strictly bound to specific data types, reducing type-related errors) and backward compatibility. It is widely used in high-performance applications, such as distributed systems, microservices and gRPC-based communication, where low latency and efficient data exchange are critical. Although less human-readable than JSON or XML, Protobuf excels in environments where performance and scalability are prioritised.

Avro

Avro is a schema-based data serialisation technology designed for efficient data storage and exchange in big data environments. It uses a compact binary format, reducing data size and improving performance, while its schema is stored alongside the data to ensure compatibility and enable schema evolution. Avro supports a variety of data structures, including arrays, maps and nested records, making it highly versatile. It is optimised for use with distributed systems such as Apache Hadoop and Apache Kafka, where it facilitates fast, efficient and consistent data processing. Avro is a popular choice in big data pipelines due to its combination of flexibility, performance and seamless integration with modern data platforms.

MessagePack

MessagePack is a lightweight, binary data serialisation format designed to efficiently store and exchange data. It is compact and faster than text-based formats such as JSON, while still maintaining compatibility with a wide range of programming languages. MessagePack is schema-less, making it flexible for dynamic data structures, and it supports complex types such as arrays, maps and nested data. Its small message size and high-speed encoding/decoding make it ideal for performance-critical applications, such as IoT devices, mobile applications and real-time communication systems, where bandwidth and processing efficiency are crucial.

Yet Another Markup Language

Yet Another Markup Language (YAML) is a human-readable data serialisation format designed for simplicity and ease of use, particularly in configuration files and data exchange. Its hierarchical, indentation-based syntax allows for clear representation of complex data structures, such as lists, maps and nested elements, without the need for extensive syntax or tags. YAML is highly compatible with most programming languages and integrates well with tools such as Kubernetes and continuous integration/continuous deployment (CI/CD) pipelines. While it is not as compact as binary formats such as Protobuf, its readability and support for comments make it ideal for scenarios where manual editing or review is required, such as application configurations and DevOps workflows.

Data processing technologies

Data processing technologies transform raw data into meaningful insights by collecting, organising, analysing and presenting it in a usable format. These technologies enable organisations to efficiently manage large volumes of data, whether through batch processing for periodic tasks, real-time stream processing for immediate insights or distributed computing for large-scale analytics. They power critical applications such as BI, ML, IoT data analysis and data integration, helping organisations to make informed decisions, optimise operations and automate and simplify workflows. Data processing technologies are essential for effectively handling complex, high-volume data environments in modern digital ecosystems.

Big data processing

Big data processing involves efficiently collecting, storing and analysing vast, complex datasets to extract meaningful insights and support decision-making in real time or batch workflows.

Popular technologies include:

- **Apache Beam**: An open-source, unified programming model for defining and executing batch and stream data processing pipelines across multiple distributed processing backends, such as Apache Spark, Flink and Google Dataflow (see *Cloud data platforms* below).

- **Apache Flink**: An open-source framework for distributed stream and batch data processing, offering high throughput, low latency and support for complex event-driven applications and real-time analytics.

- **Apache Hadoop**: An open-source framework for distributed storage and processing of large datasets across clusters of computers, using a scalable and fault-tolerant architecture.

- **Apache Kafka**: An open-source distributed event streaming platform designed for high-throughput, fault-tolerant, real-time data ingestion, processing and integration across applications and systems.

- **Apache Spark**: An open-source analytics engine for large-scale, big data processing that provides fast computations and supports batch, streaming, ML and graph processing workloads.

- **Databricks**: A cloud-based analytics platform that enables scalable data engineering, ML and collaborative data science using Apache Spark.

Extract, transform, load

Extract, transform, load (ETL) data processing involves extracting data from various sources, transforming it into a usable format and loading it into a target system (e.g. a data warehouse) for analysis and reporting.

Popular examples include:

- **Talend**: An open-source data integration and ETL platform that enables users to extract, transform and load data from various sources into target systems, supporting efficient data management and analytics workflows.

- **Apache NiFi**: An open-source data integration and automation tool designed for building scalable data flows, enabling real-time ingestion, transformation and movement of data across systems.

- **Informatica**: An enterprise data integration platform that provides tools for ETL, data quality, governance and management, enabling organisations to efficiently unify, transform and analyse data across diverse systems.

Business intelligence technologies

BI technologies enable organisations to analyse data, generate insights and create visualisations through tools such as dashboards and reports, supporting informed decision-making and strategic planning.

Popular examples include:

- **Tableau**: A popular data visualisation and analytics tool that enables users to create interactive dashboards, explore data insights and share analyses.

- **Microsoft Power BI**: A BI platform that enables users to connect, transform, visualise and share data insights through interactive dashboards and reports, seamlessly integrating with other Microsoft services.

- **Looker**: A BI and data analytics platform acquired by Google Cloud that enables organisations to explore, visualise and share real-time data insights through a flexible, SQL-based modelling layer and interactive dashboards.

- **D3.js**: A JavaScript library for creating dynamic, interactive and data-driven visualisations on the web using HTML, scalable vector graphics (SVG) and CSS.

Data science and machine learning technologies

Data science and ML technologies enable the extraction of insights, prediction of outcomes and automation of tasks by analysing complex datasets using statistical methods, algorithms and computational models.

Popular examples include:

- **Apache Arrow**: A high-performance in-memory analytics library.

- **Python**: A programming language dominant in data science, with libraries including Pandas, NumPy and scikit-learn (see below).

- **R**: An open-source programming language and software environment for statistical computing, data analysis and visualisation, widely used for its extensive library of statistical methods and graphics capabilities.

- **TensorFlow**: An open-source ML framework developed by Google, enabling the creation, training and deployment of ML and deep learning models across a variety of platforms.

- **PyTorch**: An open-source ML framework developed by Meta, known for its flexibility and dynamic computation graph, making it ideal for building and training deep learning models.

- **NumPy**: An open-source Python library that provides tools for numerical computation, including support for multidimensional arrays, mathematical functions and efficient data manipulation.

- **scikit-learn**: An open-source Python library that provides tools for ML.

- **Pandas**: An open-source Python library that provides high-performance data manipulation and analysis tools, including data structures such as DataFrames for handling structured data efficiently.

- **Dask**: An open-source Python library that enables scalable, parallelised data processing and computation on large datasets by extending tools such as NumPy, Pandas and scikit-learn to distributed systems.

Cloud data platforms

Cloud data platforms provide scalable, on-demand infrastructure and tools for storing, processing and analysing data, enabling organisations to manage and gain insights from their data without the need for on-premises (On-Prem) hardware.

Popular examples include:

- **AWS S3 (Simple Storage Service)**: A scalable, highly durable and secure object storage service by Amazon Web Services, designed for storing and retrieving any amount of data from anywhere for various use cases, including backups, data lakes and content delivery.

- **AWS Athena**: A serverless query service that enables users to analyse data stored in Amazon S3 using standard SQL, without the need to manage infrastructure or data loading processes.

- **AWS Glue**: A fully managed ETL service that simplifies data preparation and integration by automating the extraction, transformation and loading of data for analytics and ML applications.

- **Google BigQuery**: A fully managed, serverless data warehouse that enables fast, scalable analysis of large datasets using SQL, with built-in support for ML and real-time analytics.

- **Google Dataflow**: A fully managed service for stream and batch data processing, enabling scalable, real-time analytics and data pipeline development using Apache Beam.

- **Google Pub/Sub**: A fully managed messaging service that enables real-time communication between applications by asynchronously streaming events through a publish/subscribe model.

- **Microsoft Azure Synapse Analytics**: A data analytics service that integrates big data and data warehousing, enabling organisations to ingest, prepare, manage and analyse data at scale for business intelligence and ML.

- **Microsoft Azure Data Lake**: A scalable, secure data storage solution designed to handle vast volumes of structured and unstructured data, enabling advanced analytics, big data processing and ML applications.

- **Microsoft Azure Data Factory**: A data integration service that enables the creation, scheduling and coordination of data pipelines to ingest, transform and move data across diverse sources for analytics and processing.

Data governance and security

Data governance and security technologies ensure the robust management, protection and compliance of data by implementing policies, access controls and monitoring to safeguard sensitive information and maintain data integrity.

Popular examples include:

- **Collibra**: A data intelligence platform that enables organisations to manage data governance, cataloguing and privacy while promoting collaboration and compliance across their data ecosystem.

- **Alation**: A data intelligence platform that combines data cataloguing, governance and analytics to help organisations discover, understand and leverage their data for informed decision-making.

- **Apache Ranger**: An open-source framework for centralised data access governance, providing fine-grained security controls, auditing and policy enforcement across big data ecosystems.

6 CYBERSECURITY AND THE DESIGN OF SYSTEM CONTROLS

INTRODUCTION

The primary purpose of system controls is to safeguard the integrity, security and reliability of a digital solution, ensuring that it functions as intended and is resilient to security breaches, failures or misuse. Controls prevent unauthorised access, detect and address user errors, ensure compliance with policies, business rules, standards and legislation, and maintain consistent performance. The design of these controls, rather than being treated as a separate activity, should be embedded within all areas of digital solution design.

At its heart, this aspect of digital solution design revolves around addressing the questions 'What could go wrong?' and 'How can this be prevented or mitigated?' As such, the design of system controls is fundamentally about managing risks associated with the use of digital solutions. While this chapter addresses a range of risks, particular emphasis is placed on cybersecurity due to the significant impact security breaches can have on organisations and individuals.

The chapter begins by outlining various risks associated with the use of digital solutions and proceeds to examine the design of system controls that can help to prevent or reduce these risks.

RISKS ASSOCIATED WITH THE USE OF DIGITAL SOLUTIONS

In the context of digital solutions, a risk is an event that may or may not occur, which has a detrimental impact. There is a wide range of risks associated with the use of digital solutions, including:

- **Software failures**: See separate section below.
- **Cyber risks**: See separate section below.
- **Data collection and tracking**: A lack of transparency when collecting user data can lead to concerns about how this data is used and shared.
- **Loss of control**: By relying on digital solutions, users might give up some control over their personal information.
- **Data privacy**: Handling large volumes of data increases the risk of data leaks and breaches, which can compromise sensitive information and violate privacy regulations.

- **System outages**: Technical failures or system outages can disrupt access to digital solutions, impacting business operations or causing inconvenience to users.

- **Integration issues**: Integrating disparate digital solutions can be complex and lead to compatibility problems or unexpected behaviour.

- **Vendor lock-in**: Over-reliance on a specific vendor's solution can lead to lock-in, making it difficult or expensive to switch to a different provider in the future.

- **Third-party risks**: Relying on external vendors for digital solutions can expose organisations to risks associated with the reliability of those vendors and their security practices.

- **Insider threats**: Even with strong security measures, there is always a risk of malicious insiders who can misuse their access to data or systems.

- **Workforce readiness**: Implementing digital solutions might require upskilling or training for employees to effectively use them. There can be resistance to change or a skills gap that needs to be addressed.

- **Digital divide**: Not everyone has equal access to technology or the digital skills needed to use digital solutions effectively. This can exacerbate existing inequalities.

- **Algorithmic bias**: Algorithms used in some digital solutions can perpetuate biases if not carefully designed and monitored. This can lead to unfair or discriminatory outcomes.

- **Compliance risks**: Non-compliance with regulatory standards can result in legal penalties and reputational damage.

- **Operational disruptions**: Implementing new digital solutions can temporarily disrupt business processes and reduce productivity, as teams adjust to the changes.

- **Cost overruns**: Digital transformation projects can exceed budget if not carefully managed, impacting return on investment.

- **Skill gaps**: Lack of necessary skills and expertise within an organisation can hinder the successful implementation and management of digital solutions.

- **Cultural resistance**: Employees may resist changes brought by digital transformation, affecting the adoption and effectiveness of new technologies.

While all of these areas of risk should be considered and addressed during the development and deployment of a digital solution, two particular areas are especially relevant to the work of the solution designer: software failures and cyber risks. These are explored in more detail below.

SOFTWARE FAILURES

Although the term conjures up images of the complete meltdown of a computer system – 'the blue screen of death'[12] being a classic example – a software failure is a

---

12 The 'blue screen of death' (BSOD) is a critical error screen displayed by the Windows operating systems when it encounters a severe problem. It essentially indicates a system crash where Windows can no longer operate safely.

much broader concept. According to the International Software Testing Qualifications Board's (ISTQB's) *Certified Tester Foundation Level* certification syllabus (ISTQB, 2023), a software failure occurs as the result of a defect introduced through human error. It also acknowledges that failures can also be caused by environmental conditions, such as when radiation or electromagnetic fields cause defects in firmware.

In the book *Software Testing: An ISTQB-BCS Certified Tester Foundation Level Guide* (Thompson et al., 2024), one of Thompson's co-authors, Peter Morgan, provides some historical examples of software failures, which have been reproduced below with permission from BCS, The Chartered Institute for IT. *(Note: the last three examples were taken from the second edition of the book).*

- On 3 May 2021, TikTok users found they had 0 (zero) followers of their account. These things matter to a lot of people.

- When the UK government introduced online filing of tax returns, a user could sometimes see the amount that a previous user earned. This was regardless of the physical location of the two applicants.

- In November 2005, information on the UK's top ten wanted criminals was displayed on a website. The publication of this information was described in newspapers and on morning radio and television and, as a result, many people attempted to access the site. The performance of the website proved inadequate under this load and the website had to be taken offline. The publicity-created audience peaked beyond the capacity of the website.

- A catastrophic disruption of service in the Federal Aviation Authority (FAA) computer service in early 2023 resulted in services across the whole of the United States being grounded for parts of 11 January 2023.

- A new smartphone mapping application was introduced in September 2012. Among many other problems, a museum was incorrectly located in the middle of a river, and Sweden's second city, Gothenburg, seemed to have disappeared from at least one map.

- The first launch of the European Space Agency's *Ariane* rocket in June 1996 failed after 37.5 seconds. A software error caused the rocket to deviate from its vertical assent, and the self-destruct capabilities were enacted before the now-unpredictable flight path resulted in a bigger problem.

- When a well-known online book retailer first went live, ordering a negative number of books meant that the transaction sum involved was refunded to the purchaser. Development staff had not anticipated that anyone would attempt to purchase a negative number of books. Code was developed to allow refunds to customers to be made by administrative staff, but self-requested refunds are not valid.

- A small, one-line change in the billing system of an electrical provider blacked out the whole of a major US city.

Another incident that occurred since the publication of these examples is the CrowdStrike global system outage in July 2024. On 19 July 2024, CrowdStrike, a cybersecurity firm, released a faulty configuration update for its Falcon sensor software on Microsoft Windows systems, leading to approximately 8.5 million devices crashing worldwide. The update caused systems to enter boot loops or recovery modes, severely disrupting various sectors, including airlines, banks, hospitals and emergency services. CrowdStrike promptly reverted the update and issued a fix; however, many affected machines required manual intervention to restore functionality, prolonging the recovery process. The incident, deemed one of the largest IT outages in history, resulted in significant financial losses estimated at $10 billion, and prompted CrowdStrike to revise its update deployment practices to prevent future occurrences.

As explained earlier, according to the ISTQB syllabus, system failures are caused by defects introduced as a result of human error. The error could be a genuine mistake made by a developer when writing the software source code (logic errors) or they could be down to a failure by a BA, subject-matter expert (SME) or solution designer to anticipate how the system will be used.

CYBER RISKS

Cyber is a prefix that relates to, or involves, computers and computer networks, especially the internet. The term **cyber risks** therefore refers to the risks that arise from the use of computers, computer networks and the internet. More specifically, a cyber risk (also known as a **cyber threat**) is the possibility or potential of a malicious attempt to damage or disrupt a computer network, system or the information it contains. It represents the risk that a harmful event could occur, leading to the compromise of the confidentiality, integrity or availability of the target's information, resources or services. When such an event takes place, it is termed a **cyberattack**, and the risk is considered to be realised. Similar to other types of risks, the likelihood of the event occurring can be reduced through countermeasures. There are two types of countermeasure: avoidance actions (which reduce the likelihood of the risk being realised) and mitigation actions (which reduce the impact should the risk be realised).

In his book *Cyber Security: The Complete Guide to Cyber Threats and Protection* (Sutton, 2022), David Sutton cites a 2019 report on the financial cost of cyber-related fraud in the UK between April 2018 and March 2019, which estimated that £2.2 billion had been lost by victims, with 65 per cent of reports originating from businesses and 35 per cent from individuals. He concluded that:

> most people in the UK are now far more likely to be the victims of cyber crime than plain old-fashioned burglary.

Sutton describes a wide range of examples of cyber crime, which are summarised below (there is some overlap between the examples):

- **Phishing**: Deceiving users into revealing personal information through fraudulent emails or websites.
- **Identity theft**: Stealing personal information to impersonate someone and commit fraud.
- **Credit card fraud**: Unauthorised use of credit card information for financial gain.

- **Online banking fraud**: Targeting online banking systems to steal funds.
- **Ransomware**: Encrypting a victim's data and demanding a ransom for its release.
- **Hacking**: Breaking into other people's computers for fun, revenge or to make a statement of some form, often on political, ethical or environmental matters.
- **Planting the flag**: Another form of hacking where the perpetrator breaks into a system 'because they can', to demonstrate how clever they are or how poor the target's security is.
- **Exploitation**: A hacker who exploits a system they have penetrated may covertly extract data or delete or corrupt information, with serious consequences for the target organisation, system users and its customers. So-called 'data leaks' appear regularly in the media, and it is not just commercial organisations that are targeted. In May 2024 there was a data breach at the UK Ministry of Defence when a payroll system was hacked[13] and personnel data was exfiltrated. Thankfully, no operational MoD data was obtained.
- **Malware**: Malicious software designed to harm or exploit computer systems, networks or users. Malware is a catch-all term for various types of harmful software, including viruses, worms, Trojans, spyware, adware and ransomware. Cybercriminals use malware to profit financially, cause disruption or steal sensitive information.
- **Cyber espionage**: This can take two forms:
  - **State-sponsored hacking**: Governments target other countries or organisations to steal sensitive information.
  - **Corporate espionage**: Competitors steal trade secrets or intellectual property.
- **Cyber vandalism**: This can take three forms:
  - **Defacement**: A form of hacking involving the defacement of an organisation's website to show offensive images or derogatory statements about the organisation. Some hackers alter the code behind the landing page to divert users to other websites in order to extract money or plant a virus.
  - **Denial of service (DoS) attacks**: Overwhelming a system with traffic to prevent legitimate users from accessing it.
  - **Distributed denial of service (DDoS) attacks**: A more powerful version of DoS, using multiple computers to attack a target.
- **Intellectual property theft**: This can take three forms:
  - **Copyright infringement**: Unauthorised use of copyrighted material. This issue has come to the fore recently where there have been concerns about generative artificial intelligence (GenAI) applications based on large language models (LLMs) accessing copyrighted books and music as part of their training data.
  - **Patent infringement**: Using patented technology without permission.
  - **Trademark infringement**: Misusing a registered trademark.

---

13 www.bbc.co.uk/news/uk-68966497

Sutton also cites cyber harassment, cyberbullying, cyber warfare, cyber surveillance and dark patterns as other examples of cyber threats, but coverage of these is outside the scope of this book.

In order to understand cyber risks, it is necessary to first clarify some terminology.

Cyber targets

A cyber target is an entity that is the focus of a cyberattack or cyber threat. Sutton lists six general categories of cyber target:

- individuals;
- businesses;
- critical national infrastructure (communications, defence, emergency services, energy, financial services, food, government, health, transport, water and so on);
- buildings;
- academia and research; and
- manufacturing and industry.

Devices (network infrastructure and end-user devices), applications and data can also be considered to be a category, as the devices themselves are often the direct targets of cyberattacks.

Attackers (malicious actors) use a range of factors when choosing cyber targets. For example:

- **Value of data**: Systems storing valuable data, such as financial records, intellectual property (IP) or personal information, are prime targets.
- **Vulnerabilities** (see below): Organisations, individuals, systems or software with known vulnerabilities are often targeted because they offer easier access.
- **Impact potential**: Targets that, when compromised, can cause significant disruption or damage, such as critical infrastructure, are frequently chosen.
- **Access potential**: Attackers may target low-level systems or individuals as a means of gaining access to more critical targets.

Generally, the intention behind an attack is to compromise the confidentiality, integrity or availability of the target's information, resources or services by exploiting a **cyber vulnerability**.

Cyber vulnerabilities

A cyber vulnerability is a weakness or flaw in a cyber target that can be exploited to gain unauthorised access or inflict damage. According to Sutton, such vulnerabilities are the reasons why cyberattacks succeed. He identifies several categories of vulnerabilities, which are summarised in Table 6.1, with the most critical stemming from failures to establish or follow appropriate policies, processes and procedures.

Table 6.1 Cyber vulnerabilities (after Sutton, 2022)

Category	Vulnerability
Policies, processes and procedures	• Failure to have an overall information security policy • The lack of, or poorly written, access control policies • Failure to change user access rights when changing role or leaving the organisation • Inadequate user password management • The continued use of default or inbuilt system accounts and passwords • The lack of security of mobile devices • The lack of network segregation • Failure to impose a clear-desk and clear-screen policy • Restriction of administration rights usage • The use of untested software • Failure to restrict the use of system utilities • Lack of separation of duties • Inadequate network monitoring and management, including intrusion detection • The use of unprotected public networks • The uncontrolled use of user-owned wireless access points • Poor protection against malware and failure to keep protection up to date • The lack of a patching and updating regime • Inadequate and untested backup and restoration procedures • Improper disposal of 'end-of-life' storage media • The lack of robust 'bring your own device' policies • Inadequate change management procedures • The lack of audit trails, non-repudiation of transactions and email messages • Unacceptable use (lack of or non-enforcement of an acceptable use policy in employee and contractor contracts) • The uncontrolled copying of business information • Poor management of remote users

(Continued)

Table 6.1 (Continued)

Category	Vulnerability
Technical	• Poor coding practice
	• Poor specification of requirements (hence the importance of Requirements Engineering as a discipline for defining digital solutions)
	• Poor quality assurance and testing
	• Single points of failure
	• Vulnerable and outdated components
	• Poor patch management and vulnerable dependency management
People-related	• Social engineering
	• Lack of awareness or poor response to training and awareness
	• Failure to comply with company policies and good practice
	• Simple passwords
Physical and environmental	• Building and equipment room access
	• Physical access to individual items of equipment
	• Heating, ventilation and air conditioning
	• Power

Cyber impacts

The exploitation of a vulnerability during a cyberattack results in one or more cyber impacts. These are the consequences of the cyberattack. Sutton categorises these as personal and organisational impacts, as summarised in Table 6.2.

An important aspect of risk management is anticipating the impact(s) if a risk is realised, as this can help with the formulation of countermeasures.

Cyber threats and cyberattacks

As already mentioned, a cyber threat is synonymous with a cyber risk, which is essentially the probability of a cyberattack. The process for understanding the level of threat is referred to as **threat analysis**. This is concerned with determining or pre-empting the following:

- **Threat source** or **sponsor**: The person or organisation that wishes to benefit from a cyberattack.

- **Threat actor** or **agent**: The person or persons that execute an attack. The threat source often pays or pressurises the threat actor(s) to execute the attack.

Table 6.2 Cyber impacts (after Sutton, 2022)

Category	Impact
Personal	• Loss of or unauthorised changes to personal information
	• Loss of or unauthorised changes to personal credentials
	• Loss of money and other financial instruments
	• Damage to personal reputation
	• Loss of personal trust
	• Loss of or unauthorised changes to intellectual property
	• Identity theft
	• Personal injury
Organisational	• Brand and reputation
	• Financial impacts (including increasing operational costs)
	• Breach of legal obligations
	• Operational failures
	• People impacts

- **Threat action**: The attack itself. Threat actions are often not isolated events, but can consist of many discrete activities, involving surveillance, initial activities, testing and the final attacks.

- **Threat vector** or **attack vector**: A tool, technique or mechanism used to conduct the attack.

Sutton identifies the following threat actions and vectors:

- **Application layer attacks**: Take place when firewall ports are left open for an attacker to use as a means of entry.

- **Botnets**: Provide a means of targeting a large number of potential victims, most of whom are unwilling recipients. They consist of a very large number of malware-infected computers, known as 'zombies', which spread the malware that executes the attack, either generating spam email or a DDoS attack. The malware is typically installed by an unwitting user clicking on a link in a spam email or web page, which initiates the download onto the user's computer without their knowledge. Once installed, the malware allows the botnet owner to take control of the computer when they require, using one, or a group of, command-and-control computers.

- **Brute force attacks**: A cyberattacker attempts to discover something, such as a password, by testing every possible combination of characters until the correct value is found.

- **Buffer overflow attacks**: These involve breaking an application by providing it with more input than its designer expected or planned for.

- **Backdoors**: Programmers often build a 'backdoor' into their code to enable them to make changes while the code is being tested. Unless these backdoors are removed prior to the software being released, anyone who is able to find the backdoor will have instant access to the entire code to manipulate in any way they want.

- **Injection attacks**: The attacker either injects software code into a program or inserts forbidden characters that might cause an application to terminate, leaving access clear for the attacker. Three common examples of injection attacks are:

  - **SQL injection attacks**: In SQL databases, malicious SQL code (an '&' character to execute SQL commands) is injected into an application's input fields to manipulate or exploit its underlying database. By exploiting insufficient input validation, attackers can bypass authentication, retrieve sensitive data, modify or delete records or even gain full control of the database, for example an attacker might insert SQL commands into a login form to trick the database into granting unauthorised access. These attacks are among the most common and dangerous web application vulnerabilities.

  - **Command injection attacks**: These exploit improper input validation to execute arbitrary system commands on a server, typically through web applications or software interfaces. This occurs when user-supplied input is improperly handled and passed to system functions, such as shell commands or APIs, allowing attackers to manipulate system behaviour, access sensitive data or gain unauthorised control. Common attack vectors include unsanitised user input in web forms, uniform resource locators (URLs) or APIs, often leading to data breaches, privilege escalation or system compromise.

  - **Prompt injection attacks**: These target AI models, particularly LLMs, by manipulating their inputs (or prompts) to make them behave in unintended ways. These attacks occur when malicious instructions are embedded within the input data, causing the model to generate harmful or misleading outputs, override restrictions or reveal sensitive information. Prompt injection attacks highlight the vulnerabilities in AI systems relying on natural language inputs and the need for stronger validation, context awareness and safeguards to prevent misuse.

- **Network protocol attacks**: The protocols that underpin the internet, such as User Datagram Protocol (UDP) and Transmission Control Protocol/Internet Protocol (TCP/IP), are far from secure, and some attackers have been able to subvert them to cause considerable harm.

- **Rogue update attacks**: These manipulate unsuspecting or inexperienced users to download and install malware or ransomware on their computer by suggesting – typically in an email or as a pop-up on a website – that some element of the user's computer is out of date and requires an urgent update to the operating system or a commonly used application.

- **Email-borne attacks**: Software can generate email address lists extremely quickly, and emails using these addresses can be delivered rapidly and cheaply, potentially reaching thousands of email users, which is why email is an extremely common attack vector.

- **Wireless network attacks**: There are three different types of cyberattacks that use wireless connectivity:

- **Wi-Fi attacks**: Attacks on a Wi-Fi (802.x) infrastructure are extremely common and can usually be conducted in one of two ways:

    - The attacker intercepts the signal of a wireless access point, to store the intercepted data and attempt to recover the access key by 'brute force' searching.

    - The attacker introduces their own access point with a service set identifier (SSID) similar or identical to that of a genuine access point. Public spaces offering 'free' Wi-Fi are prime locations for this. When an unsuspecting user attempts to connect to the bogus access point, and provides their access key, the attacker's computer captures the data, which enables them to access the genuine network as if they were a genuine user.

- **Bluetooth attacks**: These tend to be focused on end-user devices that have their Bluetooth wireless connection enabled. When connected to the victim's device, the attacker can gain access to their address book, calendar, email and so on.

- **Global System for Mobile communication (GSM)/3G/4G/5G attacks**: Attacks against cellular mobile devices such as smartphones and tablet computers mostly use either Wi-Fi or Bluetooth as a mechanism for attacking the device, since the cellular networks use a significantly more complex key management and encryption mechanism to protect the device and its data.

- **Social media attacks**: Attacks using social media tend to focus on two distinct areas:

    - **Acquisition of personal identifiable information (PII)**: People using social media sites such as Facebook, X, Instagram, TikTok and LinkedIn frequently provide vast quantities of information about themselves, which could be used by a cyberattacker not only to gain access to their social media account, but also to enter their bank accounts and other websites.

    - **'Watering holes' and other user temptations**: Once a cyberattacker identifies a potential target on a social media site, they have the opportunity to tempt the target into accessing a website containing malware, known as a 'watering hole'.

- **Social engineering**: This typically represents a low-tech method for a cyberattacker to acquire PII or to gain unauthorised access to a computer, which may begin with a simple phone call or email to tempt or invite the individual to part with information or money, or to click on a link to a malware website, as with the watering hole example above. An alternative form of attack is where the attacker poses as a seemingly authorised person attempting to talk their way past the reception desk or gain access to a computer. Pre-'cyber', such individuals were referred to as 'confidence tricksters' or 'con artists'.

Although not explicitly cited by Sutton, another area of increasing concern is:

- **Supply chain attacks**: Adversaries target vulnerabilities in the supply chain of a product or service to infiltrate organisations. These attacks exploit trusted relationships, such as software updates or third-party services, to deliver malicious code to unsuspecting victims. One of the most notable examples is the SolarWinds attack in 2020, where hackers compromised the Orion software (a widely used IT management tool) by injecting malicious code into its updates. This allowed attackers to gain backdoor access to thousands of organisations, including major corporations and government agencies, leading to widespread espionage and data breaches. The SolarWinds attack highlighted the risks of supply chain vulnerabilities and the need for robust security measures across all stages of a product's life cycle.

AVOIDANCE AND MITIGATION OF THE RISKS ASSOCIATED WITH THE USE OF DIGITAL SOLUTIONS

As can be seen in the previous sections, there is a worryingly long and diverse set of potential risks arising from the use of digital solutions. Not all of these can be avoided or mitigated within the design of the solution – many need to be addressed at an organisational, process or person level. The POPIT model (Figure 6.1), which was introduced in Book 1 of this series, is a useful framework for considering problems and devising solutions holistically.

Figure 6.1 The POPIT model (© Assist Knowledge Development Ltd)

The POPIT model identifies five key elements that make up a business system:

- **People**: The knowledge and skills required of those working within the organisation.
- **Organisation**: The structure, culture and business model of the organisation, and the roles defined to carry out the work of the organisation.
- **Processes**: The business processes applied to carry out the work of the organisation.
- **Information**: The data and information captured, recorded and used by the organisation.
- **Technology**: The technology used to support and conduct the work of the organisation.

In order for a business system to function effectively, the five elements identified above must interact and support each other. Therefore, when focusing on one element (e.g. technology), POPIT encourages the designer to consider the impacts or issues associated with the other elements.

The solution designer's role in addressing these risks is to incorporate controls within their design that can help to avoid or mitigate the risks. These **system controls** are designed to ensure the integrity of the digital solution and its data, as well as to protect against cyber threats, and they fall into the following categories, which are explored in the next four sections:

- input and output controls;
- data controls;
- process and workflow controls; and
- security and privacy controls.

DESIGN OF INPUT AND OUTPUT CONTROLS

A significant proportion of software failures are caused by accidental user error – the wrong input of data and misinterpreted output. Inputs and outputs also represent cyber vulnerabilities. Consequently, digital solution designers must incorporate input and output controls in their designs to ensure the accuracy, security and efficiency of data entry and retrieval processes, preventing user input errors and ensuring that outputs are correctly formatted, accurate and securely delivered to the intended recipients.

Input controls

The adage 'garbage in, garbage out' (GIGO) originated in the early days of computing in recognition of a simple truth: if you input incorrect or low-quality data into a computer, you'll inevitably get incorrect or low-quality output. So, the purpose of input controls is to avoid one of the most common mistakes users of digital solutions make: mis-keying input data.

There are two categories of control that designers use to prevent incorrect data from being erroneously input into a digital solution: verification and validation. Designers also incorporate secure input mechanisms to protect applications from vulnerabilities such as injection attacks (e.g. SQL injection, command injection and prompt injection), cross-site scripting (XSS) and other malicious inputs.

Verification
Verification involves carrying out checks on input data to ensure that it has been entered or captured accurately. When designing inputs for digital solutions, the designer has at their disposal a diverse range of devices and technologies (see Chapter 3). While verification as a concept applies for any input, regardless of the technology used, clearly the precise mechanism used to verify the input data will vary depending on the input technology selected.

Perhaps the most significant challenge facing the designer when designing input mechanisms, is where the input is made by a human user – as the proverb goes: 'to err is human'. This is often referred to as **indirect data input** because it involves a human user translating source information, typically into keystrokes on a physical keyboard or touch screen. This process is referred to as **transcription**. Where a user makes a mistake during transcription (e.g. they mistype something), it is referred to as a **transcription error**.

Designers use the following techniques to detect transcription errors introduced during indirect data input, so that the user can correct them:

Double keying	The user is asked to type the same data twice and the two entries are compared. If the entries do not match, then one has been input incorrectly (a transcription error has been made) and the user is asked to rekey the data. This technique is most commonly used for critical entries such as email addresses and when creating new passwords, although it can also be used for other critical data.
Self-checking codes	A self-checking code is designed to detect transcription errors during the entry of critical codes, such as account numbers. Self-checking codes comprise two parts:

1. The base code value, which can be either a sequential number or some other faceted value (see *Design of data controls* below).

2. A check digit, which is appended to the base code value. The check digit value is calculated from the base code value using a special algorithm, such as Luhn, modulo n, weighted sum or cyclic redundancy check (CRC).

When the user inputs the code, they enter the entire code, including the check digit. The software that manages the data input then recalculates the check digit value from the base code value, using the same algorithm that was used to generate it in the first place, and compares it with the check digit value entered by the user. If the two values do not match, then a transcription error has occurred and the user will be prompted to re-enter the code.

Confirmation screens	The user is presented with the data they have just entered and asked to visually check it and confirm that it is correct. If they do not confirm, they are asked to rekey the data or correct the errors. Figure 6.2 shows an example of a basic confirmation screen for an order creation process.

In contrast to indirect data input, **direct data input** is where the input mechanism automatically translates the source information into some format that can be understood by the digital solution, without the need for human interpretation. The most common mechanisms involve scanning technologies, such as barcode or QR code scanning, optical character recognition (OCR) for interpreting handwritten or typed documents, optical mark recognition (OMR) for detecting predefined marks, or radio frequency identification (RFID). See Chapter 3 for further details regarding input technologies.

Figure 6.2 Confirmation screen from an order creation process

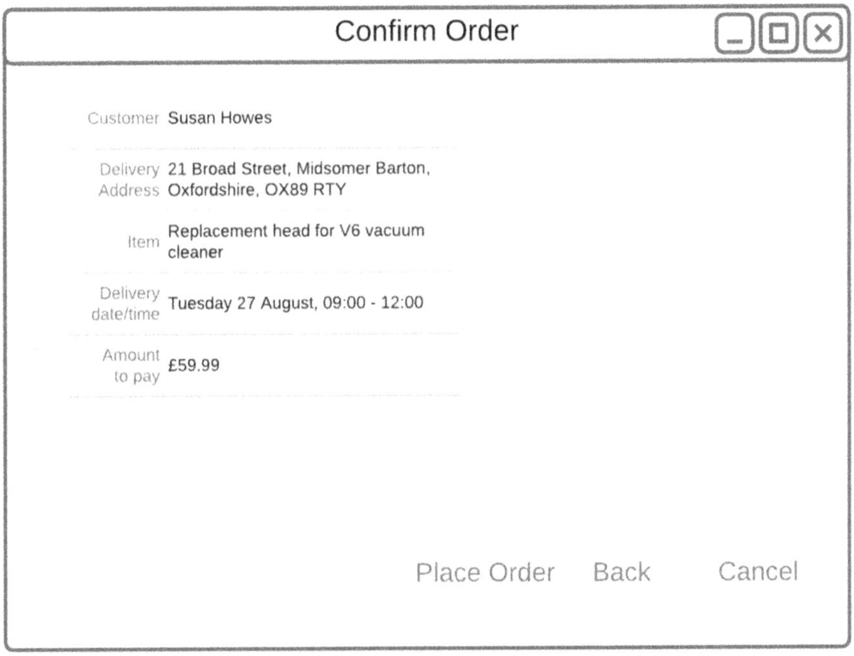

```
Confirm Order                              [_][□][×]

Customer   Susan Howes

Delivery   21 Broad Street, Midsomer Barton,
Address    Oxfordshire, OX89 RTY

Item       Replacement head for V6 vacuum
           cleaner

Delivery   Tuesday 27 August, 09:00 - 12:00
date/time

Amount     £59.99
to pay

                    Place Order    Back     Cancel
```

With the exception of self-checking codes, which can be used to detect transcription errors with both direct and indirect data input, the techniques described above are not as effective with indirect data input. For verification of indirect data input designers typically use the following techniques to detect transcription errors:

Character recognition verification	Using OCR technology to compare the transcribed data with the original image/document to identify potential errors.
Statistical analysis	Identifying outliers or anomalies in the data that may indicate errors.
Control totals	Control totals are used to verify the completeness and accuracy of data, especially during the transmission of large datasets. A number of different totals can be used, for example:

- **record count**: a count of the number of records in a dataset;
- **hash total**: the sum of values for a non-numeric field (e.g. account number) or a number field where the total is meaningless (e.g. unit price); and
- **financial total**: the sum of a numeric field with monetary values, such as the total value of orders.

Record counts and hash totals are often used as a check for the completeness of the transmitted dataset, while financial totals are used for determining the accuracy of the data transmitted. They provide a basic level of assurance that data has been processed correctly and without loss or duplication.

Control totals work as follows:

1. Before data processing, calculate the appropriate control total based on the source data.
2. Input the data into the digital solution (either directly or indirectly) and process it as required.
3. After processing, recalculate the control total based on the processed data.
4. Compare the original control total with the recalculated one. A match gives a strong indication of data completeness and accuracy.

Duplicate detection	Finding and removing duplicate entries in the input data.
Machine learning	Training algorithms to identify patterns of errors and suggest corrections.
Quality control metrics	Establishing key performance indicators (KPIs) to measure transcription accuracy.
Bar code quality assessment	Evaluating bar code clarity, contrast and damage to prevent misreading.
Error correction codes	Hamming codes and Reed–Solomon codes used to detect data transmission errors.
Random sampling	Manually verifying a random sample of scanned data to identify potential errors.

The following techniques are used specifically with RFID:

Tag read verification	Ensuring that RFID tags are read correctly and consistently.
Tag inventory checks	Verifying that all expected tags are read during a scan.
Signal strength analysis	Evaluating the strength of the RFID signal to identify potential interference or tag issues.

These verification measures are also combined with periodic equipment calibration (in the case of optical and RFID scanning) and validation checks (see below) to ensure the integrity of data inputs.

Validation

Validation, in contrast to verification, involves checking input data against rules that govern the consistency and integrity of the data to be used by a digital solution. While validation often follows on from verification, the two types of control can be combined.

Designers typically use the following techniques to validate input data, irrespective of how the data has been captured and verified:

Data type validation
Checks that each input value conforms to expected data types. For example: For an `order amount` data item, is the inputted value a real number with two decimal places? For a `customer name` data item, does the value comprise only alphabetic characters?

Length and format validation
Checks that the input value adheres to predefined formats. For example, for an `email address` data item:

- Does the local part (before the @ symbol) contain only letters (a–z, A–Z), numeric digits (0–9), periods (.), hyphens (-) and underscores (_), and not start or end with a hyphen or period?

- Does the domain part (after the @ symbol) contain at least one period and comprise only letters, numeric digits, hyphens and underscores, and not start or end with a hyphen?

- The maximum length should not exceed 64 characters.

Existence check
There are two possible existence checks:

1. For a mandatory data item, checks that the input value is not NULL. NULL is a special value that represents the absence of a value, and can be explicitly tested in most programming languages, for example 'IF `value` IS NULL'.

2. Checks that the input value (e.g. a `customer account number` or a `product code`) can be found within a master or reference data table or file.

Range check
Checks that the input value falls within a predefined range. For example, for a two-digit `order quantity` data item, is the input value a positive number between 1 and 99?

Consistency check
Checks that the input value of one data item is consistent with the input value of another, related data item. For example, in a fleet management application, check that the value of the `journey start time` data item is earlier than the value of the `journey finish time` data item. Consistency checks are also referred to as **cross-field validation**.

For some data items, multiple validation checks may be used to determine the consistency and integrity of the input data value. Additionally, when designing data entry forms, the designer may use **input masks** to constrain the values that a user can enter, to ensure that only valid values can be entered, for example an input mask for a numeric data item causes non-numeric keypresses to be ignored when the user enters the data. Input masks can also be used to automatically convert characters to upper case as the user types.

Although validation is a critical form of system control, it should be noted that incorrect validation is a common cause of defects in software systems. System designers often make incorrect assumptions about phone number formats, address formats or name formats, particularly for non-Anglophone users (someone whose primary language is not English or who does not speak English fluently). For example, requiring a customer name to be alphabetical might rule out Spanish names like 'Maria Gonzalez Garcia' (due to the space in the surname) or British names like 'Mary Grove-Bright' (due to the hyphen).

Output controls

The design of output controls involves devising appropriate mechanisms and practices to manage, monitor, secure and optimise the dissemination of information or data generated by a digital solution. The ultimate goal is to ensure that the solution delivers accurate, reliable and secure results, to the right audience, in the correct format and at the appropriate time.

A number of controls can be used by the designer to ensure the quality and integrity of the output generated by the solution, including:

Validation	In the context of output controls, validation refers to the process of ensuring that the data generated by a digital solution meets specific criteria before it is released or distributed. It's a critical step to maintain data integrity, accuracy and consistency, which involves checks similar to the input validation checks described above: • format check (e.g. checking the format against standards such as CSV (comma separated value), JSON, XML); • data type check; • range check; • consistency check; • completeness check; • accuracy check; and • compliance check – to ensure that the output complies with relevant laws, regulations and industry standards.
Monitoring	Continuous tracking of output to detect anomalies or deviations from expected patterns.
Access controls	See *Design of privacy and security controls* later in this chapter.
Data encryption	See *Design of privacy and security controls* later in this chapter.
Error handling and correction	Automated systems to identify and correct known issues or prompt users for manual correction.
Feedback mechanisms	Allowing users to report issues or provide feedback on the output, which can be used to improve the system.

Automated tools and technologies are commonly used to monitor, validate and verify outputs, reducing the risk of human error.

DESIGN OF DATA CONTROLS

The primary purpose of data controls is to ensure the confidentiality, integrity and availability of the data consumed and generated by a digital solution. These three elements are often referred to as the CIA model or CIA triad, and they form the foundation of any information management strategy, ensuring that digital information is secure, reliable and accessible.

Maintaining confidentiality, integrity and availability involves a multidisciplinary approach. From the perspective of the solution designer, their focus is on designing the following system controls:

- data quality controls;
- data privacy controls;
- data security controls.

The design of data quality controls is the focus of this section; data privacy and security controls are covered in a later section.

Data quality controls

Data quality controls primarily address the **integrity** element of the CIA triad, ensuring that data – and hence the corresponding information that is derived from it – is accurate, consistent and trustworthy, and has not been tampered with or altered by unauthorised parties. Although the latter part overlaps with data privacy and data security controls, the main focus here is on data quality.

In their publication *Data Management Body of Knowledge* (DAMA International, 2017), the Data Management Association defines eight dimensions of data quality:

- **Accuracy**: The degree to which the data correctly reflects 'real-life' entities. Measures of accuracy tend to rely on comparison of the data to a data source that has been verified as accurate.
- **Completeness**: Whether all required data is present. Completeness can be measured at the dataset, record or column level:
  - Does the dataset contain all the records expected?
  - Are the records correctly populated?
  - Are the columns/attributes correctly populated? Do all mandatory columns contain a value for each record?

  Note: the definition of correctness may be dependent on the type or status of the record.

- **Consistency**: There are a variety of different definitions/measures of data consistency, for example:
  - data values are consistently represented within a dataset;
  - data values are consistently represented between datasets;

- the size and composition of datasets is consistent between systems; and

- there is consistency of format of data values within the same column/attribute.

The first three of these are arguably more data management issues, but the last is definitely something that the designer should consider.

- **Integrity** (also referred to as 'coherence'): In the data world the most common interpretation is '**referential integrity**'. This is achieved when all foreign key values (or pointers) correctly reference an associated data object in a related dataset (table/ entity/relation) (primary and foreign keys are discussed further in Chapter 5). However, another useful interpretation is compliance with business rules (discussed below).

- **Reasonability**: This is slightly more obscure as it considers whether a data pattern meets expectations/makes sense, generally based on some benchmark data. The designer would not build in specific controls for this as it is a data quality dimension that would be measured based on the stored data.

- **Timeliness**: This refers to the currency of the data. For example, if the current position of a vehicle is not notified to a satellite navigation system in a timely way, then the system may provide an out-of-date notification to the driver to make a turn, when the vehicle has already passed the turn.

- **Uniqueness**: This refers to the lack of duplication of data.

- **Validity**: This refers to whether data values are consistent with a defined domain of values. Designers can produce domain descriptions, which contain rules that govern the attribute values for a given set of attributes, for example the rules that govern date values, which apply to all date attributes.

Some of these data quality considerations are more relevant to the discipline of IT service management (ITSM) rather than digital solution design, which is explored in Book 3 in this series, *Delivering Digital Solutions*. However, there are a number of controls that can be used by the digital solution designer to ensure data quality, including:

Data validation and verification	These techniques (discussed earlier in this chapter) help to address the accuracy, consistency, completeness and validity dimensions of data quality.
Checksums and hash functions	These enable the verification of data integrity by generating unique hash values or checksums that change if the data has been altered.
Digital signatures	These provide a way to verify the authenticity and integrity of digital messages or documents.
Version control	Tracking changes to data and ensuring that authorised modifications are properly documented.
Data normalisation	The application of a set of rules based on relational data theory to derive logically simple, redundancy-free data structures can help to achieve the uniqueness data quality by removing redundant duplication. Normalisation (see Chapter 5) aids referential integrity and also involves the design of appropriate keys that will ensure that no two rows/records in a dataset are identical.

The timeliness and integrity dimensions of data quality can also be addressed when designing process and workflow controls (see next section), where processes are specified to enforce specific business rules. These dimensions can also be addressed during data design, where data attribute definitions specify rules that govern the processing of the data (see Chapter 5).

DESIGN OF PROCESS AND WORKFLOW CONTROLS

A process is a series of structured, sequential steps designed to achieve a specific outcome, while a workflow represents the orchestration or automation of those steps, including how tasks, information and decisions flow between people, systems or components. Process and workflow controls are concerned with enforcing business rules and making sure that users of the solution are not able to perform a process or task that they are not authorised to, or to perform tasks in an incorrect sequence.

Process controls

Business rules place constraints on the activities within business processes. These are visible within the guard conditions of business process models, as can be seen in the example in Figure 6.3.

Figure 6.3 encapsulates the following rules governing payments during the order creation process of a sales order processing solution:

- If a payment is not successful, the customer shall be given the option to retry.
- If on the third attempt the payment is still unsuccessful, then the order is abandoned.
- A payment must be successful before an order can be created.

Activity diagrams were introduced in Book 1 in this series as a way of defining the process requirements for a digital solution during Requirements Engineering. Sometimes the diagram produced at this time by the BA can also be used as the process design, or instead it can be used to create a sequence diagram during process design, as shown in Figure 6.4.

In Figure 6.4 the boxes are interaction frames (also known as fragments). The Loop and Opt in the top-left cut-away part of the fragments are operators that determine the nature of the fragment. The loop fragment will repeat any interaction specified within the frame while the guard condition (shown in square brackets) is true. So if either the payment is successful or the number of attempts reaches three, the process will exit the loop fragment and continue with the next fragment.

The Ref operator is used to identify functionality defined as a separate sequence diagram, and is equivalent to the use of the ⊓ symbol in activity diagrams.

The Opt fragment is necessary to determine the circumstances that caused the loop to terminate. As has already been established, there are two possible scenarios:

1. The payment has been successful.
2. There have been three failed attempts.

Figure 6.3 Business rules in a process model

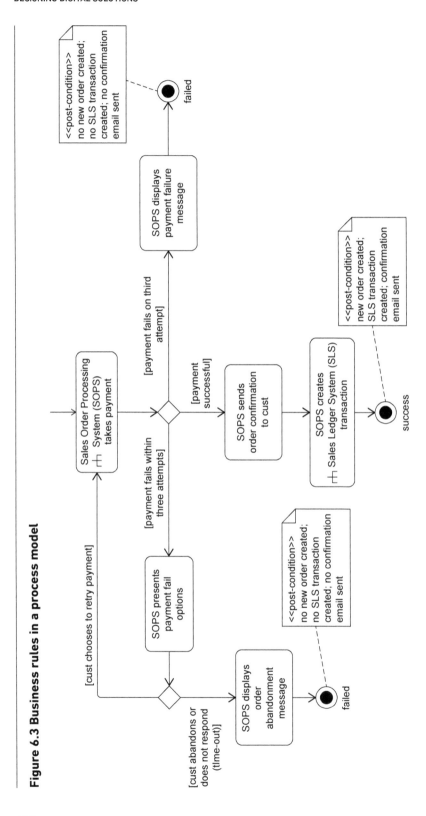

Figure 6.4 Extract from a UML sequence diagram representing business rules

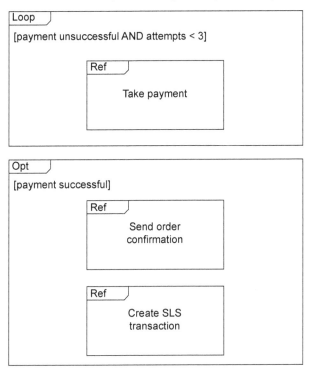

The actions within the opt fragment should only take place when the payment is successful, as determined by the guard condition [payment successful].

Workflow controls

A further type of business rule also imposes constraints on processes, but this is more the sequence in which processes, or tasks within a process, are executed, rather than conditions that must be satisfied within a process. These business rules are enforced by workflow controls, which, as the name suggests, control the flow of work.

The UML state machine diagram introduced in Book 1 is particularly useful for showing the conditions that govern the flow of work, especially in the context of core business objects, such as orders, invoices, bookings and so on. Figure 6.5 shows the life cycle of a sales order object using a state machine diagram.

The diagram shows the following workflow-related business rules:

- A successful payment must have been made before an order is authorised to be picked by the warehouse.
- If a payment has failed during the order creation process, the order is automatically cancelled.

Figure 6.5 State machine diagram: sales order object life cycle

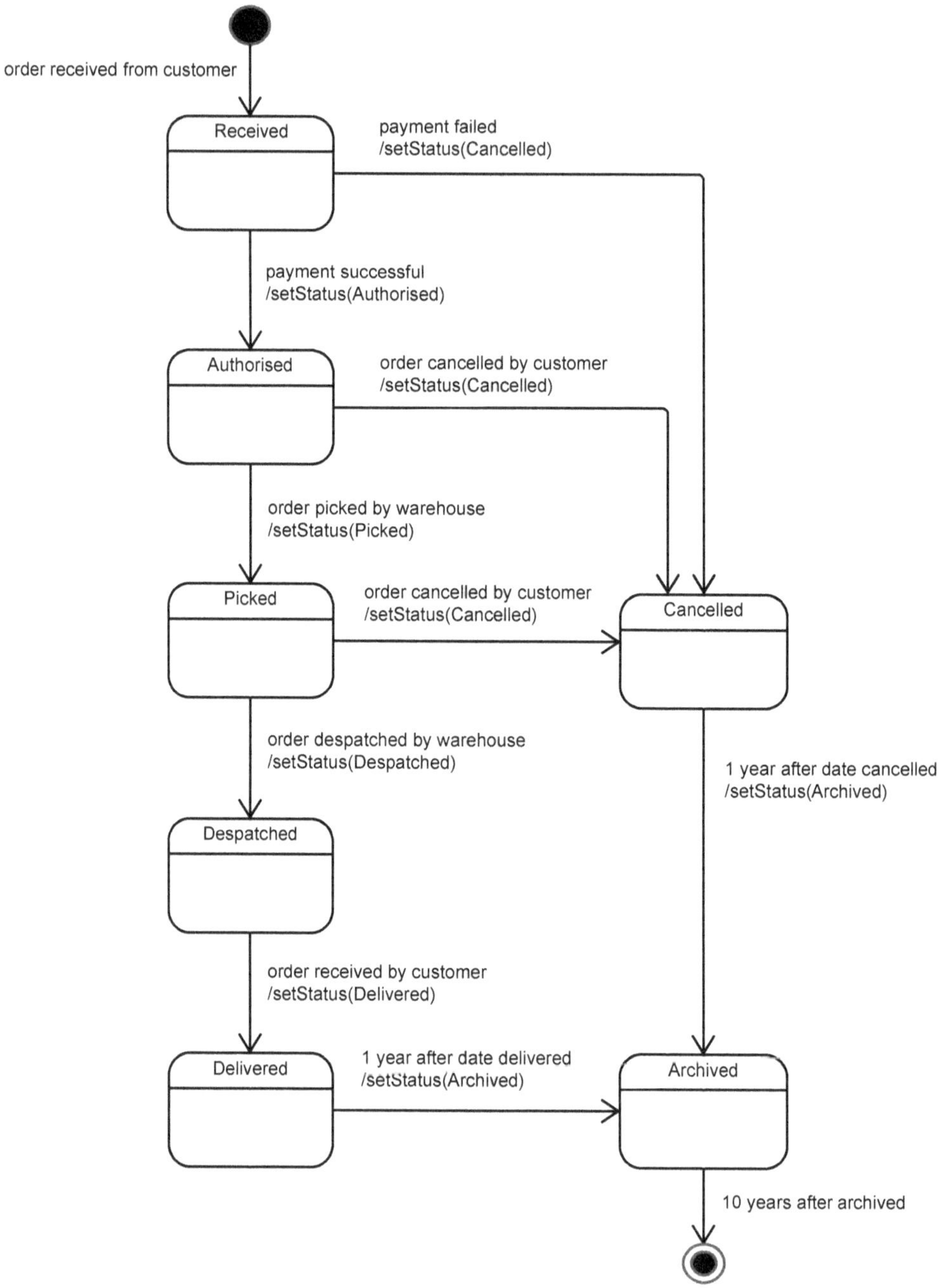

- An order must have been picked by the warehouse before it can be despatched.

- An order must have been despatched by the warehouse before it can be delivered to the customer.

- An authorised order or picked order can be cancelled by the customer prior to despatch, but an order cannot be cancelled by a customer after it has been despatched.

- Cancelled orders are automatically archived one year after the date they were cancelled.

- Delivered orders are automatically archived one year after the date they were delivered.

- Archived orders are purged 10 years after they were archived.

These rules can be implemented at both the individual object level and at the service level. Figure 6.6 shows an extract from a sequence diagram specifying the behaviour for the cancelOrder() operation for the Order class.

Figure 6.6 Sequence diagram: cancelOrder() operation

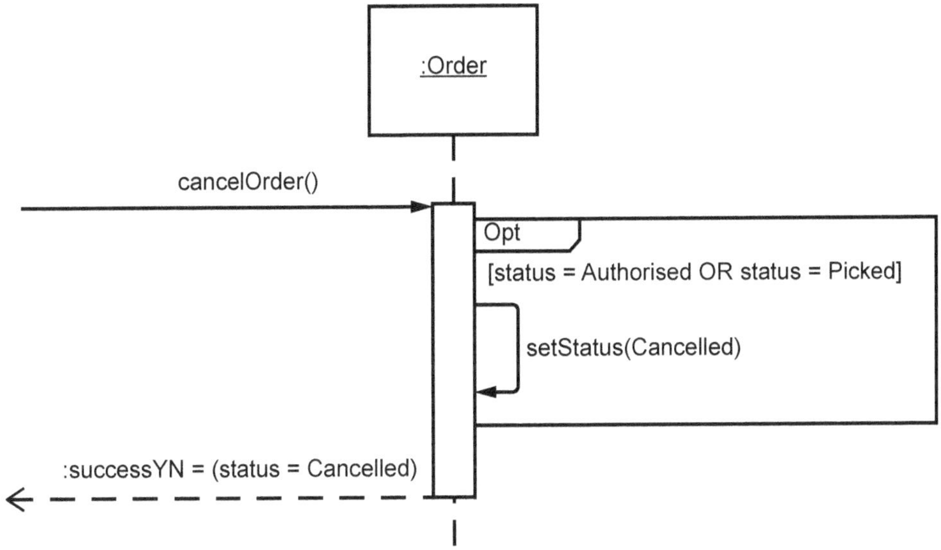

In Figure 6.6 the operation setStatus() is used to change the current status value of the object. An attempt to set the status to Cancelled is only made if the guard condition [status = Authorised OR status = Picked] is true, status being the name of the attribute within the order object that holds the current status value. The cancelOrder() operation returns a true or false value depending on the status of the object after the operation has executed. If the value of the status attribute is Cancelled, then the cancellation has been successful and the cancelOrder()

operation will return the value `True`, otherwise it will return the value `False`. The only difference between the sequence diagram for the `cancelOrder()` operation within the `Order` object and `cancelOrder()` as a service is that the latter would also need to retrieve the correct `Order` object first.

DESIGN OF PRIVACY AND SECURITY CONTROLS

Privacy and security are related concerns with shared concepts and techniques. Privacy is primarily concerned with the confidentiality element of the CIA triad and ensuring that personal data is collected, processed and shared in ways that respect individuals' privacy rights. Security, on the other hand, is concerned with ensuring that digital solutions are accessible and operational whenever required by authorised users, protecting data from unauthorised access, alteration or destruction. Security focuses on all elements of the CIA triad.

Privacy controls

When designing privacy controls, the designer's focus is on compliance with legal and regulatory requirements regarding the handling of personal information, such as the UK Data Protection Act (DPA), the European Union's General Data Protection Regulation (GDPR) and the California Privacy Rights Act (CPRA) in the United States. The CPRA superseded the California Consumer Privacy Act (CCPA) in January 2023.

While comprehensive coverage of data protection legislation is beyond the scope of this book, a key focus for the solution designer is on protecting personal identifiable information (PII) and implementing data subject rights, such as the right to:

- be informed about how their data is being used;
- access personal data held about them;
- have incorrect data updated;
- have data erased (often referred to as the right to be forgotten);
- stop or restrict the processing of their data;
- data portability (enabling the data subject to get and reuse their data for different services); and
- object to how their data is processed (in certain circumstances).

The above rights are taken from the UK DPA, but the other forms of data protection and privacy legislation have similar and equivalent rights.

Compliance with data protection and privacy legislation necessitates addressing the following considerations:

- **Data minimisation**: Collect only the personal data necessary for specific purposes and avoid unnecessary data collection. Many breaches of data protection legislation can be avoided simply by not collecting data that isn't needed.

- **Consent management**: Obtain and manage consent from individuals for the collection, use and sharing of their personal data.

- **Data subject rights**: Implement processes for responding to data subject requests, such as access, correction, deletion and portability of their personal data.

- **Transparency**: Ensure that individuals are informed about how their data is being used, typically through privacy policies and notices.

- **Purpose limitation**: Limit the collection of PII to only what is necessary for the intended purpose(s), and only use PII for the purpose(s) specified at the time of collection, unless further consent is obtained.

- **Data retention**: Establish policies to ensure that PII is not kept longer than necessary, for the purpose it was collected, and is securely deleted or anonymised when no longer needed.

While the solution designer will play an important role in ensuring compliance, it is not their sole responsibility, and they will need to collaborate with other business and technical stakeholders.

Some of the considerations listed above will translate into organisational policies and processes, such as:

- having a job role designated for handling subject access requests (SARs), with a clear process for handling such requests;

- instigating a data retention policy that necessitates that personal data be removed when no longer needed;

- displaying appropriate privacy notices; and

- classifying data based on privacy sensitivity.

Others fall within the remit of the designer and are addressed through the functional design of the solution. For example:

- To address the data subject's right to be informed about how their data is used, the designer may decide to display a specific data protection notice at the point that the data subject's data is being collected.

- To address the data subject's right to have incorrect data updated, the designer may specify a data maintenance function, possibly with self-service access, to enable the data subject to correct or update data relating to them, where necessary.

The designer may also decide to incorporate the following technical elements into the design of the solution:

- **Encryption**: Converting data into a code to prevent unauthorised access. Encryption should be applied to both data in transit and data at rest:
  - **In transit**: Encrypt PII during transmission over networks using protocols such as Hypertext Transfer Protocol Secure (HTTPS) and Transport Layer Security (TLS) to protect it from being intercepted by unauthorised parties.

- **At rest**: Encrypt PII stored on servers, databases or any storage media using strong encryption algorithms such as Advanced Encryption Standard (AES).

- **Access controls**: Implementing permissions and authentication mechanisms to restrict who can view or modify certain information. This is covered further in the next section.

- **Data masking**: Obfuscating PII by replacing it with fictional data or special characters without exposing the real data, for example displaying a series of asterisks (*) representing the end-user's keystrokes as they type a password, so that anyone nearby cannot read it.

- **Anonymisation**: Using techniques such as generalisation, pseudonymisation and data aggregation to strip PII of any identifying elements, making it difficult to trace back to an individual while still retaining the data's utility.

- **Tokenisation**: Replacing sensitive PII with non-sensitive equivalents (tokens) that can be mapped back to the original data through a secure process, protecting the actual PII from exposure.

Security controls

As with privacy, the solution designer will play an important role in maintaining security, although they are not solely responsible for it, and will need to work collaboratively with other business and technical stakeholders, to address the following considerations:

- **Access control**: Restricting access to data based on the principle of least privilege, ensuring that only authorised users can access sensitive information.

- **Encryption**: Protecting data by encrypting it both at rest and in transit (see *Privacy controls* above) to prevent unauthorised access during storage or transmission. This should also include encrypting backups (see below) and data on portable devices such as laptops and USB drives, to prevent unauthorised access if the backup media or device is lost or stolen.

- **Authentication and authorisation**: Implementing strong authentication methods, such as multifactor authentication (MFA) and ensuring that users are authorised to perform specific actions.

- **Activity monitoring**: Continuous logging and monitoring of access to data, including user activities, data access patterns and anomalies. This helps to detect unauthorised access attempts or data breaches in real time and to respond to security incidents.

- **Audits**: Conducting regular security audits and reviews of access controls, encryption methods and data handling practices to ensure they are effective and compliant with regulations.

- **Incident response**: Developing and maintaining incident response plans to quickly respond to and recover from data breaches or other security incidents.

- **Disaster recovery plans**: Maintaining a robust disaster recovery plan that includes measures for quickly restoring access to the digital solution following an outage or cyberattack. See also *backup and recovery* below.

- **Backup and recovery**: Ensuring regular backups of data with recovery plans in place, to protect against data loss due to breaches, accidents or disasters.

- **Redundancy**: Using backup systems, servers and networks to ensure continuous availability in case of a failure.

- **Adherence to standards**: Following relevant information security standards such as ISO/IEC 27001 (ISO, 2013), National Institute of Standards and Technology, Cybersecurity Framework (NIST, 2024) or National Cyber Security Centre (NCSC) guidelines (NCSC, 2023).

- **Secure coding standards**: Implementing secure coding practices to safeguard program code against cyber threats. Secure coding practices are explored further in Book 3 of this series.

- **Physical security**: Ensuring that physical devices such as servers, laptops and backup drives are stored in secure locations with restricted access. Biometric identification methods (e.g. face recognition and fingerprint recognition) also fall under physical security.

- **Security testing**: Performing regular vulnerability assessments, penetration testing and code reviews to identify and mitigate security weaknesses in applications.

While many of the above considerations stretch beyond the designer's remit, they may incorporate the following technical elements into the design of the solution to protect data from unauthorised access, disclosure, modification or destruction:

- **Encryption**: See *Privacy controls* above.

- **Firewalls**: Implementing a firewall (a security device or software that monitors and controls incoming and outgoing network traffic based on predetermined security rules) creates a barrier between a trusted internal network and untrusted external networks, such as the internet, to prevent unauthorised access and protect against cyber threats. Next-generation firewalls incorporate advanced features such as intrusion detection and prevention (see next item).

- **Intrusion protection system (IPS)**: An IPS is a cybersecurity technology designed to detect, prevent and respond to unauthorised or malicious activities within a network or digital environment. It is an essential component of a digital solution, particularly in safeguarding systems, data and networks from threats. There are two types of IPS:

  - **Network-based IPS (NIPS)**: Monitors and protects the entire network by analysing traffic as it flows across network devices.

  - **Host-based IPS (HIPS)**: Installed on individual devices (such as servers or workstations), the HIPS monitors and protects the host's activities.

- **Role-based access control (RBAC)**: RBAC is a method of managing user access to systems and resources based on the roles assigned to them within an organisation. It is a key component in ensuring security, efficiency and compliance (e.g. compliance with data protection legislation) when using digital solutions, particularly in environments where there are multiple users with varying levels of responsibility.

- **Multifactor authentication**: Implementing strong authentication methods such as MFA and ensuring users are authorised to perform specific actions adds an additional layer of security, requiring users to provide two or more verification factors to access digital solutions.

- **Least privilege principle**: Restricting access to data based on the principle of least privilege (PoLP), ensuring that users, systems, processes and applications have the minimum level of access necessary to perform their tasks and no more, thus reducing the risk of unauthorised access.

- **Data loss prevention (DLP)**: Using specialist DLP tools to monitor, detect and block unauthorised transfers of sensitive data, including PII, across networks, emails and endpoints.

- **Load balancing**: Distributing workloads across multiple systems to ensure no single system is overwhelmed. This can be an effective way of improving availability.

- **Blockchain**: Deploying blockchain distributed ledger technology (DLT) for data transactions. Blockchain provides numerous benefits to ensure transactions are secure:
  - reduced single points of failure;
  - trusted environment;
  - tamper resistance;
  - auditability;
  - end-to-end tracking;
  - security through consensus;
  - byzantine fault tolerance;
  - strong encryption;
  - digital signatures;
  - smart contracts; and
  - resistance to DDoS attacks due to its decentralised nature.

- **AI and ML**: Artificial intelligence and machine learning can be used to enhance data security through anomaly detection. This can also be used for automated responses to cyber threats. See the next section on AI and cybersecurity.

AI and cybersecurity

In recent years, AI has captured the imagination of both the public and organisations. But, as with any emerging technology, there are concerns around security.

In their article *AI and cyber security: what you need to know* (NCSC, 2024), the UK's National Cyber Security Centre issued a general warning that:

> the content produced by these tools is only as good as the data they are trained on, and the technology contains some serious flaws.

The article further explained that:

- it can get things wrong and present incorrect statements as facts (a flaw known as 'AI hallucination')
- it can be biased and is often gullible when responding to leading questions
- it can be coaxed into creating toxic content and is prone to 'prompt injection attacks'
- it can be corrupted by manipulating the data used to train the model [see *Data poisoning attacks* below].

Prompt injection attacks

According to the NCSC, prompt injection attacks are one of the most widely reported weaknesses in large language models (LLMs). They occur when an attacker creates an input designed to make the model behave in an unintended way, potentially causing it to generate offensive content, reveal confidential information or trigger unintended consequences in a system that accepts unchecked input.

Data poisoning attacks

A data poisoning attack occurs when an attacker tampers with the data that an AI model is trained on, to produce undesirable outcomes, which could include generating a biased response. The risks from these attacks are potentially growing as a consequence of LLMs being increasingly used to pass data to third-party applications and services.

Guidelines for secure AI development

The NCSC publishes a set of *Guidelines for secure AI system development* (NCSC, 2023), which are also aligned closely to the NIST *Secure Software Development Framework* (National Institute of Standards and Technology, 2022) in the United States. Detailed coverage of the guidelines is beyond the scope of this book, but they broadly mirror the stages within the life cycle of a digital solution:

- secure design;
- secure development;
- secure deployment; and
- secure operation and maintenance.

7 ARCHITECTURE AND DIGITAL SOLUTION DESIGN

WHAT IS ARCHITECTURE?

> All architecture is design, but not all design is architecture.

This is a quote widely attributed to Grady Booch, a prominent figure in the world of software engineering and one of the architects of the Unified Modeling Language (UML).

A more helpful definition, courtesy of the *Oxford English Dictionary*, is:

> The art or science of building or constructing edifices of any kind for human use.

Architecture as a human endeavour dates back to neolithic times (10,000 to 2000 BC). Of course, digital solutions were thousands of years away at this time but, although architecture as it applies to the design of buildings is very different to the kind of architecture that applies to digital solutions, they have one thing in common – both concern the overarching design of a solution to meet a particular human need.

A useful definition of architecture from a digital solution perspective can be found in the ISO/IEC/IEEE 42010:2022 standard (ISO, 2022d):

> Fundamental concepts or properties of a system in its environment embodied in its elements, relationships, and in the principles of its design and evolution.

As can be seen from this definition, architecture is quite an abstract concept, but it does relate to some more concrete things: the elements and relationships of a system, and principles that guide its design and evolution.

As with design, the term architecture can be used to refer to both the 'human endeavour' – the process of defining and building architectures – and the deliverables of this endeavour – the architecture descriptions or blueprints produced along the way.

In the context of digital solutions, architecture (the endeavour) refers to the structured framework used to conceptualise, design and manage the components, interactions and underlying infrastructure of digital solutions, which can encompass everything from software applications to entire IT ecosystems, ensuring that they are functional, scalable, secure and aligned with business goals. A key objective of anyone undertaking this work is to determine the most appropriate way in which to represent the architecture descriptions, and this is often in the form of documentation containing an appropriate set of models.

In his book *Solution Architecture Foundations* (Lovatt, 2021), Mark Lovatt describes an architectural approach to solving problems that is:

> strategic, holistic and progressive ... an alternative to applying tactical 'quick fixes' that are short-term and narrowly focused.

Lovatt's approach involves:

- seeing the big picture of a problem, including how it may be solved **conceptually**;
- breaking the problem down into components and making models to see how they work together **logically** to solve the problem; and
- itemising the **physical** changes that are required to move from problem to solution, possibly in incremental stages.

ARCHITECTURE GRANULARITY

Architecture granularity refers to the level of detail or specificity in the design of a system, which determines how much breakdown and refinement is applied to the components of the system, and their interactions. In this context, 'system' can refer to any type of system, including business systems and IT systems.

In the context of digital solution design, high granularity means that the solution is broken down into many smaller, more finely grained, components, which can lead to increased flexibility, improved maintainability and greater scalability. However, it also means increased complexity – therefore, highly granular architectures are more difficult to understand and more challenging to manage.

In contrast, low granularity means that the solution is divided into fewer, larger and more coarsely grained components, which can lead to reduced complexity (fewer components to manage) and improved performance (fewer interactions between components can lead to faster execution). However, low granularity can also lead to decreased flexibility (changes to a large component may impact the entire system) and reduced scalability (scaling the solution may require changes to the overall architecture).

The concept of granularity can also be applied to the different levels of architecture. The following levels are considered in this chapter:

- enterprise architecture (low, coarsely grained);
- solution architecture (medium); and
- software architecture (high, finely grained).

ENTERPRISE ARCHITECTURE

Enterprise architecture (EA) is the highest level and most holistic form of architecture, concerning an organisation (the enterprise) as a whole, over a strategic time frame. The organisation in question can be a huge, global multinational employing hundreds of thousands of employees all over the world and operating in many geographical marketplaces, or it can be a small family-run business. One is clearly a lot more complex than the other, but fundamentally both are business systems with similar features. For example, both have:

- a context or environment within which they exist;
- a mission – the reason why they exist;
- a set of products and/or services that they provide to a customer base;
- an organisational structure with individuals fulfilling roles;
- a set of processes that are executed to realise an operating model; and
- information and data that they process and maintain about their organisation, for either their own purposes or to meet legal and compliance requirements.

Ideally, all organisations (enterprises) should have a vision of what they want to be in the future to remain relevant to their customers. This will necessitate evolving through changes to meet the challenges presented by a constantly changing business environment, which in turn requires a strategy to achieve that over a period of time.

Enterprise architecture is primarily concerned with these highest level, long-term, strategic issues. The individual changes conducted to support this strategy can usually be seen as shorter-term, tactical changes, which is where **solution architecture** comes in.

Enterprise architecture domains

According to The Open Group Architecture Framework (TOGAF), there are four core enterprise architecture domains (The Open Group, 2022):

- business architecture;
- data architecture;
- application(s) architecture; and
- technology (infrastructure) architecture.

In addition to these core domains, TOGAF also recognises other cross-cutting areas such as **security architecture** and **governance**, which influence and integrate across the primary domains. These domains, when effectively aligned, provide a comprehensive blueprint for organisations to achieve their strategic objectives while optimising IT investments and operations.

Each EA domain represents a subset of the overall enterprise architecture. The domains are interconnected and share areas of overlap, as illustrated in Figure 7.1.

Figure 7.1 Enterprise architecture domains (© Assist Knowledge Development Ltd)

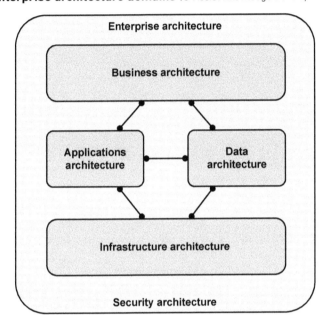

In Figure 7.1, 'Applications architecture' actually refers to two distinct but related forms of architecture: 'application**s** architecture' (plural) is described below with the other domains, but 'application architecture' (singular) is synonymous with software architecture, which is described in a later section.

Business architecture

There are numerous definitions of business architecture in common use, but one that has gained particular traction is the definition provided by the Business Architecture Guild (2024) in their body of knowledge:

> Business architecture represents holistic, multidimensional business views of: capabilities, end-to-end value delivery, information, and organizational structure; and the relationships among these business views and strategies, products, policies, initiatives, and stakeholders.

This is quite an academic definition. In more straightforward terms, business architecture is a structured discipline that involves understanding and designing the structure and behaviour of a business system, aligning its operations and strategies with its goals and objectives. It focuses on how a company's resources, capabilities, information and processes interact to achieve business outcomes and helps to create a clear connection between strategic goals and operational execution, ensuring that the business operates efficiently and can adapt to changes.

Data architecture	Data architecture is focused on the definition and design of how data is shared, collected, stored, moved, used and managed within and outside an organisation, throughout its life cycle. A data architecture comprises enterprise-wide definitions of the data required to support the information needs of the organisation and its applications, to enable data-driven decision-making and to ensure that the right data is available to the right people at the right time.
Applications architecture	Applications architecture concerns the definition and design of the overall structure of all software applications used by an organisation. It provides a high-level view of how different applications are organised, integrated and deployed to ensure that applications integrate well with each other, and the portfolio of applications aligns to business objectives and supports business needs efficiently, while considering factors such as performance, scalability, security and maintainability. It also serves as a strategic tool for decision-making, ensuring that applications can scale and evolve over time in alignment with business goals and technological advancements.
Infrastructure architecture	Infrastructure architecture concerns the design and organisation of the physical and virtual components that support the operations of an organisation's IT environment, in alignment with business strategy. It involves the planning, structuring and management of hardware, software, networks and data centres that form the backbone of all technology systems and services, and provides the technical platforms upon which digital solutions are deployed. In essence, the infrastructure architecture ensures that hardware, software and networks work together cohesively and provide a robust, scalable and secure foundation that supports business applications, data and user needs while ensuring reliability, compliance, performance and resilience.
Security architecture	Although security is arguably an integral part of each EA domain, some organisations consider security architecture as a domain in its own right, providing a holistic approach that cuts across the other domains to ensure end-to-end security, meeting the business security needs and policies. Cybersecurity (see Chapter 6) is a subset of this, focusing on the information systems and infrastructure elements.

Typical artefacts produced within each core domain are listed in Table 7.1.

Table 7.1 Typical architecture artefacts (by domain)

Domain	Artefact	
Business architecture	• Business capability model • Business capability heat map • Business process models (BPMs) • Organisational structure diagram • Business strategy document • Value stream map • Customer journey map • Balanced scorecard • Business motivation model • Strengths, weaknesses, opportunities, threats (SWOT) analysis	• Business glossary • Product and service catalogue • Stakeholder map • Operating model • Ecosystem map • Business use cases • Governance framework • Roadmap for business transformation • Gap analysis • Business Requirements Document (BRD)
Data architecture	• Data inventory or data catalogue • Data flow diagram (DFD) • Conceptual data model • Logical data model • Physical data model • Canonical data model • Reference data model • Entity–relationship diagram (ERD) • Data dictionary • Data life cycle diagram • Master data management (MDM) artefacts • Data governance framework	• Data interaction architecture diagram • Data warehouse or data lake architecture • Data lineage diagram • Data quality reports • Data access and security policies • Metadata model • Data retention and archival policy • Big data architecture • Data reporting and analytics architecture • Data APIs and service documentation
Applications architecture	• Application portfolio inventory • Application landscape diagram • Application component diagram • Application interaction diagram • Data flow diagram (DFD)	• Application roadmap • Service-oriented architecture (SOA) models • Technology stack diagram • Security architecture documents • Business process model

(Continued)

145

Table 7.1 (Continued)

Domain	Artefact	
	• Logical application architecture diagrams	• API documentation and specifications
	• Physical application architecture diagrams	• Performance and capacity planning artefacts
	• Use case diagrams	• Application life cycle documentation
	• Sequence diagrams	• Gap analysis document
	• Application deployment diagram	
Infrastructure architecture	• Infrastructure architecture diagram	• Infrastructure as code (IaC) blueprint
	• Network topology diagram	• High availability (HA) architecture diagram
	• Physical data centre diagram	• Infrastructure life cycle management document
	• Cloud infrastructure diagram	• Integration architecture diagram
	• Server inventory and configuration document	• Infrastructure roadmap
	• Storage architecture diagram	• Backup and archiving strategy
	• Virtualisation architecture diagram	• Service-level agreement (SLA) documentation
	• Disaster recovery (DR) architecture	• Infrastructure risk assessment report
	• Capacity planning and performance monitoring artefacts	• Compliance and regulatory documentation
	• Infrastructure security architecture	• Cloud adoption framework

SOLUTION ARCHITECTURE

Enterprise architecture is strategic and guides evolutionary changes to the whole enterprise over a period of time. Many of those individual changes will require the oversight of a solution architecture, which is a more tactical form of architecture focused on solving a particular business problem, typically related to selected digital solutions and business processes.

A solution architecture will include a subset of elements found within an enterprise architecture, and therefore solution architecture effectively cuts across all EA domains, but its scope is limited to the solution under investigation, as reflected in Lovatt's definition, which has been adopted by the *BCS Foundation Certificate in Architecture Concepts and Domains* syllabus as follows:

Solution architecture focuses on a specific business problem or opportunity within a specific system, which may include elements from multiple domains. It should be recognised that architecture may include elements other than IT, such as people or manual processes.

Solution architecture is a discipline concerned with the production and management of a blueprint for a comprehensive solution, that addresses a business need, problem or opportunity, and integrates with the business, in alignment with its strategy, while minimising negative impacts.

(Lovatt, 2021)

The term 'solution architecture', like other forms of architecture, is used to refer to both the documentation (the blueprint as mentioned in the above definition) describing the structure and behaviour of a solution to a business problem, as well as the process for describing the solution and the work to deliver it.

Figure 7.2 provides a useful overview of the relationship between EA domains and solution architecture.

Figure 7.2 Relationship between EA domains and solution architecture (© BCS, The Chartered Institute for IT)

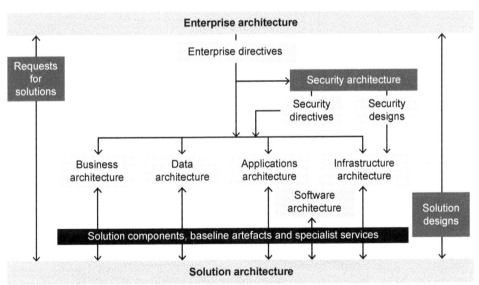

Initially, the solution architecture provides a high-level overview of the solution's building blocks, including IT and non-IT elements, and how they interact to meet the requirements. This outlines the work for more detailed design (as described in Chapters 3–6) and implementation, which then needs to be overseen or governed by the solution architect. Any need to change any of the requirements or building blocks is analysed by the solution architect to determine the impact across the architecture and resolve any issues.

The granularity of a solution architecture is often still not at the lowest level of detail possible – it defines key components or building blocks of a solution that need to be implemented, some of which may already exist and be reused.

SOFTWARE ARCHITECTURE

Often confused with solution architecture, software architecture (also referred to as 'application architecture', as distinct from 'application**s** architecture') defines how the application components, defined at a high level in the solution architecture, can be implemented by more granular software components.

Again, Lovatt's definition of software architecture has been adopted by the *BCS Foundation Certificate in Architecture Concepts and Domains* syllabus:

> The development and documentation of the structure and behaviour of a software system or component including its internal and external interfaces.
>
> (Lovatt, 2021)

The BCS syllabus also defines the following objectives for software architecture:

- Produce effective and efficient designs that satisfy organisational requirements.
- Ensure modularity of software that promotes interoperability and reuse.
- Ensure software service complies with service-level agreements.
- Ensure software is maintainable and can be modified when business needs change.

These objectives align to the objectives of digital solution design introduced in Chapter 1.

Not only does software architecture provide a blueprint of the structure and behaviour of a software system, which shows how the various components of the system interact with each other to realise functional and non-functional requirements, it also concerns the principles guiding its design, development and evolution.

Software architecture is not static; it evolves over time as new requirements emerge and technology advances, so it is essential for architects to periodically review and update the architecture to ensure that it continues to meet the needs of the business and its users.

Software architecture artefacts

Software architecture artefacts are documents and models that describe the structure and behaviour of a software system, and the interactions between the components that make up the system. They provide a shared understanding between architects, developers and business teams and serve a variety of different purposes, including:

- They are essential tools for designing, documenting and communicating the structure and behaviour of a software system.

- They help stakeholders to plan, design, implement and manage software solutions, while ensuring that these solutions meet functional and non-functional requirements, and align with business and technical objectives.

- They provide a clear direction for implementation of a software system, ensuring consistency, quality and adherence to design principles.

- They act as reference materials throughout the software development life cycle (SDLC), helping teams to understand design decisions, dependencies and limitations.

- They identify potential risks, such as performance bottlenecks or security vulnerabilities, early in the design process.

- They facilitate future enhancements, updates and troubleshooting by providing a clear view of a software system's designed structure and behaviour.

- They ensure that a software system is built according to clear, well-defined principles and requirements.

Typical artefacts produced as part of software architecture are listed in Table 7.2. Many of these are standard notations defined within the UML.

Table 7.2 Typical software architecture artefacts

Artefact	Purpose
Architecture overview diagram	• Provides a high-level view of a software system, showing the major components, modules, services and the interactions between them. • Helps stakeholders to understand the system's overall structure and key design decisions.
Component diagram (UML)	• Identifies a software system's components and shows how different parts of the system (such as modules, services and libraries) are connected and how they interact to perform specific functions. • Useful for identifying reusable components and understanding dependencies between modules.
Class diagram (UML)	• Describes the structure of a software system in terms of its classes, attributes, methods and relationships (inheritance, association, aggregation and composition). • Commonly used in object-oriented design to model the static structure of the system.

(Continued)

Table 7.2 (Continued)

Artefact	Purpose
Sequence diagram (UML)	• A form of interaction diagram that shows how the objects or components of a software system interact with one another in a particular sequence to perform a task or realise a use case. • Helps to illustrate the flow of data and control between components over time.
Use case diagram (UML)	• Represents the interactions between actors (users or external systems) and a software system to achieve specific goals, defining an overview of the main functionality provided by the system and its behaviour from a user's perspective.
Deployment diagram (UML)	• Depicts the physical deployment of software components on hardware or cloud infrastructure, illustrating how components (e.g. databases, application servers, web servers) are distributed across nodes, networks and data centres.
Data flow diagram (DFD)	• Represents how data moves through a software system, including inputs, processing, storage and outputs. • Useful for understanding how information is processed, shared and transformed within the system.
Database schema diagram	• Describes the structure of a database, including tables, relationships (primary and foreign keys) and constraints, that provides persistent data storage for a software system. • Helps developers to understand how data is stored, queried and maintained.
State machine diagram (UML)	• Describes the states of a software component or object and the transitions between these states, triggered by specific events. • Useful for modelling software systems where objects pass through various states during their life cycle (such as order processing).
API documentation	• Provides detailed descriptions of a software system's application programming interfaces (APIs), including endpoints, input/output data, authentication and usage examples. • Essential for developers integrating with the system or building services on top of existing functionality.
Logical architecture diagram	• Focuses on the abstract, logical layers of a software system (e.g. its presentation, business logic and data layers), and how these layers interact. • Helps to separate concerns and organise the system into manageable parts.

(Continued)

Table 7.2 (Continued)

Artefact	Purpose
Physical architecture diagram	• Describes the actual hardware, networking and storage components required to support a software system. • Includes details such as servers, load balancers, firewalls and data storage devices.
Communication diagram (UML)	• Similar to sequence diagrams, communication diagrams focus on the interaction between software components or systems, showing how messages flow between them to complete a process. • Useful in understanding system interactions in service-oriented or microservices architectures.
Configuration diagram	• Provides an overview of the configuration settings of a software system, including software versions, environment variables, dependencies and third-party integrations. • Important for ensuring that different environments (e.g. development, staging, production) are configured consistently.
Non-functional requirements (NFR) documentation	• Defines the non-functional requirements for a software system, including performance, scalability, security, reliability and availability, which provides clear guidelines and constraints that the system must adhere to while meeting functional requirements.
System context diagram	• Represents a software system in the context of its external entities, including users, other systems, and data sources. • Shows the boundaries of the system and how it interacts with entities within its wider solution ecosystem.
Error handling and logging diagram	• Describes how a software system handles exceptions, errors and logging mechanisms. • Important for understanding how failures are managed, logged and monitored in production.
Security architecture diagram	• Highlights the security controls and mechanisms within and in support of a software system, such as firewalls, encryption, authentication and access controls. • Ensures that the system is designed with appropriate security measures to protect data and maintain integrity.

(Continued)

151

Table 7.2 (Continued)

Artefact	Purpose
Technical debt documentation	• Describes areas where shortcuts or compromises have been made during the design and/or development of a software system, leading to technical debt. • Helps business and technical stakeholders to understand and prioritise areas that may require refactoring or improvements in the future.
Service-oriented architecture (SOA) diagram	• Represents the services, service contracts and message flows in a service-oriented software system. • Helps to understand how individual services interact and collaborate to provide end-to-end functionality.
Microservices architecture diagram	• Represents the decomposition of a software system into independent microservices, detailing how they communicate (such as using REST or message queues) and how they are deployed. • Useful for large, scalable systems where services are developed and deployed independently.
Event storming diagrams	• Visualises the flow of events in an event-driven software system, showing how components react to events and how data flows through the system. • Often used in event-driven or microservices architectures to model asynchronous communication.
Application roadmap	• A timeline that outlines the phases of development, deployment and upgrades for a software application. • Helps to track progress, dependencies and milestones in the SDLC.
Governance and compliance documentation	• Defines the standards, regulations and best practices a software system must comply with. • Ensures that the software adheres to legal and regulatory requirements.
Change management plan	• Describes how changes to the architecture will be proposed, reviewed and implemented. • Includes documentation of the process for handling updates, feature additions and refactoring.

THE ROLE OF SOFTWARE ARCHITECTURE IN DIGITAL SOLUTION DESIGN

At the beginning of this chapter, 'architecture' was described as 'overarching design', with enterprise architecture being the overarching design of an enterprise, solution architecture being the overarching design of a solution (incorporating both IT and non-IT solution building blocks) and software architecture being the overarching design of any software elements of the overall, holistic solution. Software architecture is therefore an essential element of digital solution design, providing a structured approach to making key technical decisions that align technical solutions with business goals, while ensuring that the solution can meet both the immediate and long-term needs of the commissioning organisation and its customers.

The choices made by software architects shape the digital solution and often involve trade-offs between competing priorities, such as scalability versus performance, or flexibility versus simplicity. These decisions are critical to ensuring the digital solution meets the business and technical requirements while being feasible to build and maintain.

The artefacts produced by software architects are the blueprints that guide and govern the design, development, deployment and maintenance of software systems, in particular a level of design below software architecture that is part of software development, as explored in Chapters 3–6.

There are a number of benefits from having a solid software architecture as a basis for digital solution design:

- **Alignment with business goals**: Ensures that software architecture supports long-term business objectives and can adapt to changes in business strategy.

- **Consistency**: Ensures that all software systems within an organisation adhere to the same design and development practices, thus reducing complexity.

- **Quality**: Promotes best practices and proven methodologies to ensure high-quality software that is reliable, scalable and maintainable.

- **Efficiency**: Streamlines development processes by providing clear guidelines, reducing the need for ad hoc decision-making and speeding up project delivery.

- **Risk mitigation**: Reduces the risk of security breaches, performance bottlenecks and costly technical debt by enforcing policies and standards.

- **Scalability and performance**: Provides a foundation that supports growth in users, data and functionality without significant degradation in performance.

- **Maintainability and flexibility**: Promotes code and software structures that are easy to understand, modify and extend, enabling developers to add new features, fix defects or refactor code without breaking the software system or requiring significant re-work.

- **Team collaboration**: By clearly defining the structure and responsibilities of different components, software architecture enables teams to work in parallel on different parts of the software system.

- **Security and reliability**: Architectural decisions, such as using secure communication protocols, role-based access control or redundancy, can ensure that the software system is resilient and secure against failures or attacks.
- **Communication**: Provides a common language for developers, architects, stakeholders and management to discuss the design of a software system, ensuring everyone is aligned on how the system should work and be built.
- **Reuse**: Encourages code reuse and use of standard components, reducing the time to market and improving consistency across applications.

Many of these benefits (and the design objectives discussed in Chapter 1) are outlined through architectural policies and principles (discussed below) that guide all software development projects. Additionally, target hardware and software constraints are often determined by an organisation's overarching strategy, which may include pre-established supply, support and maintenance agreements with preferred vendors. This ensures consistency and avoids project teams independently making decisions that could lead to higher costs and increased support and maintenance overheads.

SOFTWARE ARCHITECTURE POLICIES, PRINCIPLES AND STANDARDS

Software architecture policies, principles and standards are fundamental guidelines that promote consistency, quality and alignment between technology and business objectives in the design, development, management and evolution of software systems. They play a crucial role in ensuring that systems meet both business goals and technical requirements, contributing significantly to the realisation of the benefits outlined earlier.

Policies

Policies are formal rules or directives that govern the design, implementation and management of software architecture within an organisation. They set boundaries and define the responsibilities of architects, developers and other stakeholders.

Table 7.3 identifies a set of common software architecture policies and describes their purpose.

Principles

Principles are fundamental concepts that guide architectural decisions at all levels. In software architecture, they shape the design and evolution of systems to align with business goals, ensure future readiness and support maintainability and scalability. They also help to address the key concerns of major stakeholders.

Table 7.4 identifies a set of common software architecture principles and describes their purposes.

Table 7.3 Typical software architecture policies

Policy	Purpose
Compliance policy	Ensures that software adheres to legal, regulatory and organisational requirements, such as data protection legislation (e.g. GDPR).
Security policy	Defines security standards that must be embedded in the architecture, such as encryption, authentication and authorisation protocols, as well as guidelines for protecting against vulnerabilities.
Technology selection policy	Establishes criteria for selecting approved technologies, platforms and frameworks to ensure compatibility, reduce technical debt and avoid unnecessary complexity.
Code quality and review policy	Sets standards for code quality, review processes and version control practices. This ensures that code is maintainable, reliable and free of critical defects.
Cloud and infrastructure policy	Provides guidance on the use of cloud services, data centres and infrastructure to ensure scalability, reliability and cost efficiency.
Performance and scalability policy	Defines performance benchmarks and guidelines for scaling the software to handle future load increases.
Change management policy	Outlines how changes to the architecture (such as adding new features or making upgrades) should be handled, including review processes, documentation requirements and impact assessments.

Table 7.4 Typical software architecture principles

Principle	Purpose
Separation of concerns	Different components or layers of the software should focus on distinct aspects of functionality, making it easier to maintain, understand and modify the system.
Single responsibility principle (SRP)	Each module or component should have a single responsibility and one, and only one, reason to change. This principle ensures that components are modular and easier to understand, test and maintain (it is easier to locate and fix defects and add new features). Additionally, components designed with SRP are more likely to be reusable in other parts of the application or in different projects, as they focus on one specific area of functionality and can be easily adapted.

(Continued)

Table 7.4 (Continued)

Principle	Purpose
Loose coupling	Components should be as independent as possible, so changes in one part of the software do not have unintended consequences in another part. This leads to increased resilience, flexibility and maintainability.
High cohesion	Related functionality should be grouped together within a module or component to reduce complexity and increase reusability.
Scalability first	Software should be designed in a way that enables scaling both horizontally (adding more servers) and vertically (upgrading existing servers).
Reuse before build	Where possible, reuse existing code, services or third-party components instead of building from scratch, to save time, reduce defects and improve consistency.
Encapsulation	Internal details of components should be hidden from the rest of the software, exposing only necessary interfaces. This ensures that changes within components do not affect other parts of the software.
Don't repeat yourself (DRY)	Repeated logic should be avoided by centralising common functionality, which reduces errors and improves maintainability.
Fail fast and recover	Systems should detect problems early (fail fast) and have mechanisms for fast recovery, ensuring high availability and resilience.
Security by design	Security should be built into the architecture from the beginning, not added as an afterthought.
Evolvability and flexibility	The architecture should be designed to accommodate change easily, ensuring that future enhancements and modifications can be made without major disruptions.

Standards

Standards are specific, prescriptive guidelines that dictate how software is designed, developed and deployed. They ensure consistency across projects and teams and often refer to best practices, coding guidelines or tools.

Table 7.5 identifies a set of common software architecture standards and describes their purpose.

Table 7.5 Typical software architecture standards

Standard	Purpose
Coding standards	• **Languages and frameworks**: Define the approved programming languages, libraries and frameworks (e.g. Java, .NET, Python) to be used across the organisation.
	• **Code style guidelines**: Specify coding conventions such as naming conventions, indentation and code formatting to ensure readability and maintainability (such as Google's Java Style Guide and Python PEP 8).
	• **Error handling and logging standards**: Establish guidelines for handling exceptions and logging errors consistently across a software system for debugging and auditing purposes.
Design and modelling standards	• **Unified Modeling Language (UML)**: A standardised way to visually model and represent the architecture, including class diagrams, sequence diagrams and component diagrams.
	• **Entity–relationship diagrams (ERDs)**: A standard representation for modelling data and database design, ensuring consistency in how data relationships are captured.
	• **REST API design standards**: Define standards for designing APIs, including endpoint naming, HTTP methods, response codes and payload structures for REST-based architectures.
Security standards	• **Open Web Application Security Project (OWASP) Top 10**: Compliance with OWASP's security guidelines (OWASP Foundation, 2021) to address the most critical web application security risks.
	• **Encryption standards**: Define minimum encryption requirements for data at rest and in transit (such as AES-256 for data encryption, TLS for data transmission).
	• **Authentication and authorisation**: Standards for implementing security protocols such as OAuth, OpenID Connect and JWT for user authentication and role-based access control (RBAC).
Data standards	• **Data formats**: Approved data formats (such as JSON, XML and CSV) ensure consistent data serialisation across software systems.
	• **Data integrity and validation**: Standards for ensuring that data entered or processed is accurate, consistent and validated.
	• **Data storage and access**: Guidelines on how and where data should be stored (such as relational versus NoSQL databases) and accessed (such as using object-relational mapping (ORM) or direct queries).

(Continued)

Table 7.5 (Continued)

Standard	Purpose
Infrastructure and deployment standards	• **CI/CD pipeline standards**: Define how continuous integration and deployment processes should be set up, including tools (such as Jenkins and GitLab CI) and version control practices (such as Gitlow).
	• **Infrastructure as code (IaC)**: Standards for automating infrastructure provisioning using tools such as Terraform, Ansible and AWS CloudFormation.
	• **Containerisation**: Best practices for using containerisation technologies such as Docker, and orchestration tools such as Kubernetes, to deploy scalable and portable applications.
	• **Monitoring and alerting standards**: Define tools and practices for system monitoring (e.g. Prometheus and Grafana) and setting up automated alerts for critical issues.
Testing standards	• **Unit testing**: Minimum requirements for unit tests to ensure code correctness at the function or class level.
	• **Integration testing**: Guidelines for testing interactions between different components, modules or services.
	• **Performance testing**: Standards for load and stress testing, defining acceptable levels of performance, response times and resource usage.
	• **Security testing**: Minimum security testing standards, including penetration tests and vulnerability scans.

SOFTWARE ARCHITECTURE PATTERNS

The concept of patterns was first introduced in Chapter 2 in the context of design patterns. Software architecture patterns are similar in concept to the design patterns described in Chapter 2, but the main difference between them lies in their scope and level of abstraction. Design patterns focus on solving common, recurring coding problems within individual components or modules of an application, by providing solutions in terms of how best to structure or organise the program code at the class or object level. In contrast, software architecture patterns provide established, well-defined solutions to common design challenges regarding the high-level structure of the entire application or software system, defining the organisation of software components, their relationships and how they interact at a broader level, usually across subsystems, components or modules, to handle higher-level challenges such as scalability, maintainability and performance.

There are several benefits arising from the use of software architecture patterns, including:

- **Improved maintainability**: By following established patterns, code becomes more modular and easier to understand for developers working on a software development project. This makes future maintenance and modifications less error-prone.

- **Scalability and performance**: Many patterns are designed to address scalability concerns, allowing the system to grow and handle increased demands efficiently, or to guide decisions that optimise performance.

- **Reduced development time**: Using proven patterns as a foundation can save time compared to designing from scratch, enabling developers to focus on implementing the required functionality of the software system.

- **Communication and collaboration**: Architectural patterns provide a common language for developers to discuss the software system's structure and behaviour, promoting better communication and collaboration within the development team.

There are numerous software architecture patterns in current use, each suited to specific situations. Table 7.6 provides a brief summary of some of the more popular patterns.

Table 7.6 Popular software architecture patterns

Pattern	Description
Monolithic architecture	This pattern refers to a traditional software architecture style where the entire application is built as a single, unified unit. In a monolithic architecture, all components of the software – such as the user interface (UI), application (business) logic and data access layers – are tightly integrated and run as a single executable. This means that the entire application is deployed and scaled as a single package, often referred to as a monolith.
Client–server architecture (CSA)	This pattern separates the application logic and data storage (server) from the user interface (client), enabling easier maintenance and scalability as the client and server can be independently developed and deployed. CSA is ideal for simple applications where a client needs to interact directly with a server to access functionality or data.
Component-based architecture (CBA)	With this pattern the software system is decomposed into independent, reusable and self-contained components. Each component is a modular unit that encapsulates a specific functionality or set of related functionality and interacts with other components through well-defined interfaces. CBA focuses on separating concerns, promoting reusability and making systems easier to maintain and scale.
Layered architecture	This pattern organises the system into distinct layers, each with a well-defined purpose, such as the presentation layer, business logic (application) layer and data access layer. This promotes modularity and separation of concerns.

(Continued)

Table 7.6 (Continued)

Pattern	Description
	There are two common examples of a layered architecture:
	• **Three-tier**: Comprises three distinct layers – presentation, application (business logic), and data (data access) – where each layer runs on separate infrastructure components.
	• *n*-**tier**: An extension of the three-tier architecture that introduces more layers (tiers), such as caching, business services and external services, to further separate concerns.
Service-oriented architecture (SOA)	Often regarded as an evolution of CSA (see above), SOA structures applications as a collection of loosely coupled, independent, reusable services that communicate over a network using standardised protocols (HTTP, SOAP and REST). Each service is designed to perform a specific business function and can interact with other services to complete tasks or processes. SOA allows organisations to break down complex applications into smaller, reusable services, which enhances flexibility, scalability and maintainability.
	While similar to CBA (see above), the primary difference lies in their scope, purpose and the way they structure and organise software. While both architectures aim to promote modularity and reuse, they operate at different levels of abstraction and are intended for different types of systems (see Table 7.7 below).
Microservices architecture	This pattern breaks down the application into small, independent services that communicate with each other, thus promoting modularity, flexibility and independent deployment of services.
	SOA and microservices architecture share some similarities, such as focusing on creating loosely coupled, independent services. However, there are key differences:
	• **Granularity**: Microservices are typically more finely grained than SOA services. Each microservice performs a smaller, more focused task, while SOA services can be broader and more comprehensive.
	• **Communication**: SOA often relies on enterprise service buses (ESBs) or middleware for communication between services, which can introduce more complexity and coupling. Microservices tend to use lightweight communication protocols (such as HTTP/REST) and avoid centralised orchestration.
	• **Independence**: Microservices are designed to be more autonomous and independently deployable, whereas SOA services might be more dependent on other services or centralised infrastructure.

(Continued)

Table 7.6 (Continued)

Pattern	Description
Event-driven architecture (EDA)	With this pattern, the flow of an application is determined by events, which are state changes or significant occurrences within a software system. In an event-driven architecture, components communicate by producing and consuming events, often exchanging messages asynchronously, thus promoting loose coupling between components, that are reactive to changes in real time, making this pattern particularly suited to real-time applications.
Model view controller (MVC)	This pattern separates an application into three interconnected components: the model (data and business logic), the view (UI) and the controller (coordination and control): • **Model**: Represents the data and the business logic of the application. It manages the data, responds to requests for information, and notifies the view or controller when data changes. • **View**: Responsible for displaying the UI and presenting the data provided by the model to the user. It defines what the user sees on the screen and is updated whenever the model changes. • **Controller**: Acts as the intermediary between the view and the model. It processes user input (such as button clicks or form submissions), updates the model and determines which view should be displayed based on the interaction. MVC is a powerful and widely used architecture for structuring applications, particularly in web development. It promotes the separation of concerns by organising code into the model, view and controller layers, making the software system more maintainable, scalable and testable. While MVC introduces complexity in smaller applications, it is extremely beneficial for large-scale systems where maintaining a clear division between UI, business logic and data management is crucial.
Model view viewmodel (MVVM)	An architectural pattern that separates the UI (view) from the business logic (model) using a middle layer (viewmodel) that binds the data to the UI. • **Model**: Represents the data and business logic of the application. It is responsible for managing data, handling business rules and interacting with databases or external services. • **View**: Responsible for defining the UI and presenting data to the user. It binds to properties and commands exposed by the viewmodel, making it possible to update the UI automatically when data changes.

(Continued)

Table 7.6 (Continued)

Pattern	Description
	• **Viewmodel**: Acts as a middle layer between the view and the model. It exposes data and commands (e.g. button actions) to the view through properties and methods, and handles UI logic (such as validation and input processing). The viewmodel communicates with the model and updates the view using data binding.
	By separating concerns into model, view and viewmodel, MVVM enhances the maintainability, testability and flexibility of applications, while also leveraging data binding to reduce the complexity of updating the UI. Though it introduces some overhead and complexity, MVVM is ideal for applications with rich and dynamic UIs where decoupling UI logic from business logic is crucial.

Each software architecture pattern serves different needs depending on the complexity, scalability requirements and modularity of the system being built. Monolithic and client–server architectures are simpler and suitable for smaller applications, while SOA, microservices and event-driven architectures cater to large-scale, distributed and cloud-native solutions. Layered, three-tier and *n*-tier architectures offer structured, scalable designs for enterprise applications, while component-based, MVC and MVVM patterns focus on modularity and separation of concerns, especially in UI-driven solutions.

Table 7.7 provides a more detailed comparison of the patterns identified in Table 7.6. It should be noted that there is some overlap between patterns.

INTERACTIONS BETWEEN COMPONENTS AND SERVICES

The communication methods used in the architecture patterns listed in Tables 7.6 and 7.7 differ based on the architecture's goals, level of abstraction, level of coupling and need for synchronous or asynchronous interactions. Although this book does not cover each method in detail, Table 7.8 outlines the communication styles and technologies used in each pattern.

MODEL-DRIVEN ARCHITECTURE

Model-driven architecture (MDA) is a software design and development approach centred around the use of models to automate the development of software systems. MDA was introduced by the Object Management Group (OMG) and aims to separate the business logic and system functionality from the underlying technical implementation, enabling developers to focus on the design of the software system without being tied to specific platforms, languages or technologies.

Table 7.7 Software architecture pattern comparison

Pattern	Key features	Advantages	Disadvantages	Use cases
Monolithic	• Tightly coupled components • Deployed and scaled as a single unit • Simpler development in early stages	• Simple to develop and deploy for small applications • Fewer components to manage, making it easier to debug and test	• Hard to scale specific parts independently • Can become unwieldy and difficult to maintain as the application grows • Entire application must be redeployed for any change	Simple small to medium-sized applications with low complexity
Client–server	• Two components: client and server • Server manages resources, processes requests and returns data • Common in web and desktop applications	• Simple and effective for straightforward client–server interactions • Centralised control makes management easier	• Scalability issues as the number of clients increases • The server can become a single point of failure	Web applications, mobile apps and desktop apps that rely on centralised data or functionality
Layered	• Clear separation of concerns • Layers include presentation, business logic and data access • Typically uses synchronous communication between layers	• Easy to maintain and test since each layer is self-contained • Enhances modularity and promotes separation of concerns	• Can lead to performance bottlenecks as requests pass through multiple layers • Not flexible for complex workflows requiring cross-layer communication	Enterprise systems and applications with clear separation of concerns

(Continued)

Table 7.7 (Continued)

Pattern	Key features	Advantages	Disadvantages	Use cases
Three-tier	• Three layers (tiers): presentation layer (UI), application layer (business logic) data layer (database) • Each layer runs on separate infrastructure components	• Clear separation between UI, application logic and data • Each tier can be scaled independently	• Complex deployment • Network latency between tiers can slow down the system	Web applications, enterprise software, systems requiring independent scaling of front-end, logic and data
N-tier	• Similar to three-tier, but with additional layers such as middleware or external services • Can involve asynchronous communication	• More scalable and flexible than three-tier • Each tier can be optimised independently	• More complexity in design and deployment • Latency increases with the number of tiers	Complex enterprise applications, distributed systems, high-traffic systems requiring more flexible scaling and modularity
Component-based	• Components encapsulate functionality and communicate through interfaces • Promotes reuse of components across different applications	• Enhances modularity and reusability • Easier to maintain and test individual components	• Complexity in managing component dependencies • Component interaction can lead to performance overhead	Large systems requiring modular design, desktop apps, frameworks with reusable UI components
Service-oriented	• Services communicate over a network, often using HTTP, SOAP or REST • Loosely coupled and reusable services	• Services can be reused across multiple applications • Flexible and scalable, as each service can be developed, deployed and updated independently	• Complex governance and management of services • Communication overhead due to network-based interactions	Large-scale enterprise systems, business process automation, systems requiring cross-platform integration

(Continued)

Table 7.6 (Continued)

Pattern	Key features	Advantages	Disadvantages	Use cases
Microservices	• Services are small, independent and loosely coupled • Each microservice has its own data store and life cycle • Often uses REST or messaging for communication between services	• Highly scalable and flexible; each microservice can be updated, deployed and scaled independently • Enables faster development cycles with smaller teams	• High operational complexity (managing numerous services, monitoring, debugging) • Network overhead due to service-to-service communication	Large-scale, complex applications with independent, modular services (such as Netflix and Amazon)
Event-driven	• Events trigger actions in different parts of the system • Loosely coupled components that react to events • Asynchronous communication model	• Highly scalable and responsive to changes in real time • Loose coupling allows components to evolve independently	• More complex to design and debug due to asynchronous communication • Potential for event handling latency	Real-time systems, IoT applications, financial systems and systems requiring high scalability and responsiveness (such as stock trading platforms and sensor networks)
MVC	• Model handles data and business logic • View is responsible for displaying data • Controller processes user input and interacts with the model	• Clear separation of concerns • Easier to maintain and update UI independently from business logic	• Overhead in managing the interaction between components • Can become complex in large applications	Desktop applications and web frameworks (such as Ruby on Rails and Django)
MVVM	• Viewmodel exposes data and commands to the view • Two-way data binding between viewmodel and view	• Enhanced testability of the business logic • Clean separation of UI and business logic, making UIs easier to maintain	• Can become complex due to heavy use of data binding • Overhead in managing data synchronisation between viewmodel and view	Commonly used for building UIs, particularly in desktop and mobile applications using Windows Presentation Foundation (WPF) and Xamarin, Universal Windows Platform (UWP) and Avalonia.

Table 7.8 Communication methods used in software architecture patterns

Pattern	Communication method
Monolithic	Direct method calls, shared memory
Client–server	Request–response over network (HTTP, TCP/IP)
Layered	Layer-to-layer, API/method calls
Three-tier	API/method calls between presentation, business and data tiers
N-tier	Method calls, APIs, messaging between multiple tiers
Component-based	Interface-based communication (method calls, message passing)
Service-oriented	Network protocols (HTTP, SOAP, REST), middleware (ESB)
Microservices	RESTful APIs, gRPC, messaging (Kafka, RabbitMQ)
Event-driven	Asynchronous events via event brokers or message queues
MVC	Direct calls between controller and view/model
MVVM	Data binding between view and viewmodel, method calls to model

In MDA, models are considered the core components of software development and the transformation of models from one level of abstraction to another is semi-automated. There are three types of model, each at a different level of abstraction:

- **Computer (or computation)-independent model (CIM)**: The highest level of abstraction, which represents the system in terms of the business requirements and processes, capturing high-level functionality and user interactions without regard to the system's internal behaviour or technology platform.

- **Platform-independent model (PIM)**: Abstracts system functionality without considering the specifics of any particular platform.

- **Platform-specific model (PSM)**: A more detailed model tailored to a specific platform or technology stack (e.g. Java, .NET, cloud infrastructure) based on the PIM. This enables the same PIM to be used to create web, mobile, desktop and cloud implementations.

Code generation tools take the PSM and automatically generate executable code for the target platform, ensuring that the system's implementation aligns with its high-level models.

MDA uses a four-stage process, which is summarised in Figure 7.3:

1. Create a CIM.

2. Develop a PIM.

3. Transform PIM into PSM.

4. Generate code from PSM.

Figure 7.3 Overview of the MDA process

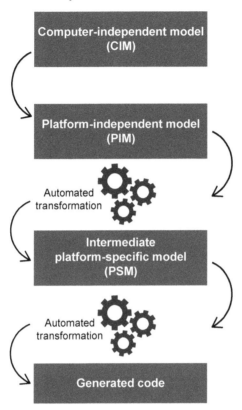

MDA offers organisations and development teams the following benefits:

- **Increased abstraction**: MDA allows developers to focus on high-level design and functionality rather than low-level coding details. By separating concerns, teams can work on business logic without worrying about the underlying technical platforms.

- **Portability and reusability**: Since the PIM is platform-independent, it can be reused across multiple platforms by generating different PSMs, leading to faster development of multi-platform applications.

- **Consistency and automation**: The automated transformation of models ensures that the generated code stays consistent with the original design, reducing the risk of human error and improving the reliability of the system.

- **Rapid adaptation to new platforms**: When new technologies or platforms emerge, the solution can be adapted to the new environment by creating a new PSM for that platform, without the need to redesign the entire solution from scratch.

- **Better communication with stakeholders**: Models (CIM and PIM) promote better communication between technical teams and non-technical stakeholders, as models can be more easily understood than code.

However, there are also some noticeable disadvantages:

- **Tool dependency**: The success of MDA depends heavily on the availability and quality of tools for model transformation and code generation. Not all tools provide full automation, and some may require manual intervention.

- **Complexity in modelling**: Developing accurate and detailed models, particularly for large and complex systems, can be difficult and time-consuming. It requires a solid understanding of both modelling techniques and the application and technology domains.

- **Lack of flexibility in generated code**: While automated code generation provides consistency, it may not always result in the most optimised or flexible code. Developers may need to manually refine the generated code in some cases, especially for performance or specific technical requirements.

- **Learning curve**: Teams unfamiliar with MDA may face a steep learning curve, especially in adopting model-driven tools and practices. Modelling languages such as UML and understanding the transformation process can take time to master.

8 SOFTWARE TOOLS TO SUPPORT DIGITAL SOLUTION DESIGN

INTRODUCTION

Designing effective digital solutions requires more than creativity and technical know-how – it demands the use of the right tools to streamline processes, enhance collaboration and ensure high-quality outcomes. AI tools are increasingly being utilised to support the design of digital solutions by enhancing efficiency, improving accuracy and promoting creativity.

This chapter explores a range of software tools that support the design of digital solutions. By leveraging these tools effectively, organisations can optimise their processes, reduce development time and deliver impactful digital solutions.

The main tools can be grouped as follows, with some overlap across categories:

- collaboration tools;
- backlog management tools;
- document management tools;
- systems modelling tools;
- UI and UX design tools;
- data design tools;
- risk management and security tools;
- generative design tools;
- documentation tools;
- CASE tools.

Some of the tools explored in this chapter are common to defining digital solutions, and have been reproduced from Book 1 for completeness.

A brief description of each category of tool with a summary of their key features and example products is provided below. Not all tools provide all features of their category and the list of specific tools is not exhaustive.

COLLABORATION TOOLS

Collaboration tools play a vital role in promoting effective teamwork by enabling seamless communication, coordination and idea sharing among team members. Designed to boost productivity and innovation, these tools empower remote and in-office teams to collaborate smoothly and efficiently, ensuring everyone remains informed and aligned.

Typical features provided by collaboration tools include:

- real-time messaging and video conferencing;
- digital whiteboards for brainstorming;
- file sharing and integration with other tools; and
- task tracking and commenting for collaborative work.

Typical examples of collaboration tools include: Microsoft Teams, Slack, Miro, Mural, Google Workspace, Dropbox, Asana and Notion.

BACKLOG MANAGEMENT TOOLS

Backlog management tools assist teams in effectively organising, prioritising and tracking tasks or features throughout the development process. These tools provide a centralised platform to manage requirements, user stories and defects, ensuring transparency and clear visibility of what needs attention. By ranking tasks based on urgency or value, they help designers and developers to focus on critical work that aligns with project objectives. Additionally, they promote collaboration by enabling team members to update progress, share feedback and assign responsibilities in real time, thereby enhancing productivity, minimising miscommunication and ensuring the final solution meets user and stakeholder expectations.

Typical features provided by backlog management tools include:

- Agile and Kanban boards for visualisation and prioritisation of tasks and features;
- backlog refinement and dependency tracking;
- integration with development workflows and tools; and
- iteration planning and burndown charts for monitoring team progress.

Typical examples of backlog management tools include: Jira, Trello, Azure DevOps, Wrike and ClickUp.

DOCUMENT MANAGEMENT TOOLS

Document management tools are essential for centralising, organising and securely managing digital documents. They facilitate efficient document retrieval and collaboration, helping development teams to streamline workflows, maintain compliance and reduce dependence on paper-based processes.

Typical features provided by document management tools include:

- version control;
- role-based access;
- advanced search and metadata tagging;
- collaboration with commenting and real-time updates; and
- compliance with regulatory standards.

Typical examples of document management tools include: SharePoint, Google Workspace, Box, Alfresco, M-Files, Notion and DocuWare.

SYSTEMS MODELLING TOOLS

Systems modelling tools help designers to visualise, analyse and test complex systems before they are built. They make it easy to create diagrams and other artefacts that represent the structure, processes and interactions within a digital solution, illustrating how different parts work together. By identifying potential inefficiencies, dependencies and bottlenecks early in the design stage, systems modelling tools help to optimise workflows and reduce costly errors. They also facilitate collaboration by providing a shared framework for discussing and refining system architecture. Ultimately, these tools enhance decision-making, improve system reliability and ensure the digital solution aligns with business and user requirements.

Typical features provided by systems modelling tools include:

- support for UML, business process model and notation (BPMN) and Systems Modeling Language (SysML) notations;
- simulation and validation of system designs;
- integration with requirements management and software development tools; and
- advanced visualisation for system architecture.

Typical examples of systems modelling tools include: Enterprise Architect (Sparx Systems), MagicDraw, IBM Engineering Systems Design Rhapsody, Microsoft Visio and MATLAB/Simulink.

UI AND UX DESIGN TOOLS

UX and UI design tools facilitate the design process by enabling the creation of wireframes, prototypes and high-fidelity mock-ups that emulate user interactions. These tools promote real-time collaboration, optimise workflows and maintain consistency in design elements. UI-specific tools, often integrated within UX platforms, concentrate on visual components such as typography, colour palettes and layout. By effectively utilising these tools, designers can improve usability, boost user satisfaction and deliver a seamless experience across different devices.

Some of the more commonly used UI and UX design tools are described below.

Storyboarding tools

Storyboarding tools enable designers to visually outline user journeys, interactions and workflows, creating a clear narrative of how users will interact with a digital solution. These tools assist in illustrating scenarios, highlighting key touchpoints and identifying potential pain points to ensure that designs align with user needs and expectations. By providing a visual framework, storyboarding tools enhance collaboration among stakeholders, simplify decision-making and bridge the gap between conceptualisation and implementation. They play a crucial role in developing user-centred designs that emphasise functionality, accessibility and an intuitive user experience.

Typical features provided by storyboarding tools include:

- drag-and-drop interface for creating storyboards;
- pre-designed templates for quick visualisation;
- annotation tools for describing scenes and sequences; and
- collaboration features for team reviews.

Typical examples of storyboarding tools include: Storyboard That, Canva, StoryBoarder and Milanote.

Wireframe tools

Wireframe tools enable designers to create simplified, low-fidelity representations of a digital solution's layout and structure. These tools help to outline the placement of key elements such as navigation menus, buttons and content areas, ensuring a clear visual hierarchy and logical flow. By focusing on functionality and user interactions rather than detailed visuals, wireframe tools enable designers to experiment, iterate and validate ideas early in the design process. They also facilitate collaboration among team members and stakeholders, helping to align expectations and lay a strong foundation for developing user-centred and intuitive interfaces.

Typical features provided by wireframe tools include:

- drag-and-drop elements for wireframe design;
- pre-made UI components for quick layout creation;
- export options to share with stakeholders; and
- collaboration and version control features.

Typical examples of wireframe tools include: Figma, Adobe XD, Balsamiq, InVision and Axure RP.

Prototyping tools

Prototyping tools enable designers to build interactive, high-fidelity mock-ups that replicate the appearance and functionality of the final product, supporting teams in the testing of user interactions, functionality and overall usability before development starts. These tools provide a platform to explore design concepts, collect feedback from users and other relevant stakeholders and refine ideas to address potential issues. By bridging the gap between static wireframes and the finished solution, prototyping tools play a crucial role in creating engaging, user-focused digital experiences.

Typical features provided by prototyping tools include:

- interactive design elements for user flow testing;
- real-time collaboration and feedback;
- support for clickable prototypes to simulate user experiences; and
- integration with design and development tools.

Typical examples of prototyping tools include: Figma, Adobe XD, Balsamiq, InVision and Axure RP.

AI design assistants

AI design assistants use AI to simplify and improve the UI design process, providing capabilities such as automated layout creation, design recommendations and user behaviour forecasting. These tools can evaluate existing designs, streamline workflows and suggest enhancements based on industry standards or user insights. By handling repetitive tasks such as resizing elements and aligning components, AI design assistants free up time for designers to concentrate on creativity and innovation. Additionally, they can anticipate user preferences and evaluate usability, enabling the efficient development of intuitive, user-focused designs.

Typical examples of AI design assistants include: Figma's AI plugins, Adobe Sensei and Uizard.

Accessibility testing

Accessibility testing tools play a vital role in ensuring digital solutions are inclusive and accessible to users with varying abilities. They help to identify issues such as inadequate colour contrast, missing alt text or non-compliant navigation, enabling designers to address these barriers early in the design process. By automating evaluations against standards such as WCAG, these tools streamline the identification of accessibility issues and provide actionable recommendations. This empowers teams to create designs that are both inclusive and compliant with regulations, ensuring they are equitable and user-friendly, and deliver an enhanced overall user experience.

Typical examples of accessibility testing tools include: Deque Axe, WAVE, Lighthouse and Microsoft Accessibility Insights.

Heatmap and behaviour analysis

Heatmap and behaviour analysis tools provide insights into how users interact with a digital solution by visualising user behaviour through heatmaps, click maps and scroll maps, highlighting areas of high engagement or potential friction. These tools also track behavioural patterns, such as navigation paths or time spent on specific elements, helping designers to identify usability issues and optimise layouts. By leveraging these insights, teams can make data-driven decisions to refine designs, improve user experiences and ensure the interface aligns with user needs and expectations.

Typical examples of heatmap and behaviour analysis tools include: Hotjar, Crazy Egg and Mouseflow.

DATA DESIGN TOOLS

Data design tools enable designers to structure, organise and visualise data effectively, assisting with the development of data models, establishing relationships between datasets and ensuring consistency in how data is managed and accessed. By providing visual representations like database schemas or interactive dashboards, data design tools make it easier to plan for scalability, optimise performance and ensure the solution supports user and business needs. They also facilitate collaboration between designers, developers and other stakeholders, ensuring the digital solution is underpinned by a robust and efficient data architecture.

AI-driven data design tools leverage AI to automate data modelling, optimise database structures and generate insights, enabling faster, more accurate and scalable data solutions tailored to user and business needs.

Data modelling

AI-driven data modelling tools utilise AI to automate the creation, optimisation and analysis of data models, streamlining complex processes and reducing manual effort. These tools can identify patterns, suggest relationships between datasets and ensure models are scalable, efficient and aligned with business requirements. By offering real-time insights and recommendations, AI-driven tools help development teams to address potential issues early, improve data accuracy and enhance overall performance. They also enable faster decision-making and promote collaboration between designers, developers and other business and technical stakeholders, ensuring the data architecture supports both user and organisational needs.

Typical examples of AI-driven data modelling tools include: ER/Studio Data Architect and IBM Data Modeler.

Database optimisation

AI-driven database optimisation tools leverage artificial intelligence to enhance database performance by automating tasks such as query optimisation, indexing and workload analysis. These tools analyse usage patterns, identify inefficiencies and provide recommendations to improve speed, scalability and resource utilisation. By proactively detecting bottlenecks and suggesting adjustments, AI-driven tools help to ensure databases operate efficiently, even under heavy loads. They also simplify maintenance, reduce manual intervention and support the delivery of robust, high-performing digital solutions.

Typical examples of AI-driven database query optimisation tools include: Aiven AI Database Optimizer, DBmarlin, EverSQL and SQLAI.ai.

RISK MANAGEMENT AND SECURITY TOOLS

Risk management and security tools help to identify, assess and mitigate potential risks while ensuring robust protection against security threats. These tools enable teams to conduct vulnerability assessments, monitor for breaches and enforce compliance with security standards and regulations. By integrating features like threat detection, risk scoring and real-time alerts, they enable designers and developers to address vulnerabilities early in the design process. This proactive approach ensures that digital solutions are not only secure and resilient, but also align with user trust and organisational requirements for data protection and risk minimisation.

Typical examples of risk management and security tools include: ProjectManager, StandardFusion, RSA Archer and LogicManager.

GENERATIVE DESIGN TOOLS

Generative design tools use algorithms and AI to create optimised solutions based on specific parameters and goals. Tools such as Autodesk Generative Design, Fusion 360 Generative Design and DeepAI help designers to quickly explore options, streamline workflows and develop creative, functional designs. By automating complex tasks and offering data-driven suggestions, these tools enhance efficiency and support innovative approaches in areas such as interface design, system architecture and user experience. Additionally, frameworks such as TensorFlow, PyTorch and Google Vertex AI enable developers to build custom AI models, enabling organisations to improve workflows, boost reliability and create tailored digital solutions for business and user needs.

DOCUMENTATION TOOLS

Documentation tools facilitate the creation, organisation and sharing of technical and project-related information. Generic tools such as Confluence help teams to collaboratively document requirements, workflows and design decisions, ensuring alignment to business needs and transparency, while specialist tools such as Swagger/OpenAPI and Postman focus on specific technical needs such as defining and documenting APIs (Swagger/OpenAPI) and testing and monitoring APIs throughout the development process (Postman). Together, these tools streamline collaboration, improve communication among stakeholders and ensure that digital solutions are well-documented, maintainable and aligned with project goals.

COMPUTER-AIDED SOFTWARE ENGINEERING TOOLS

Computer-aided software engineering (CASE) tools streamline and automate essential stages of the software development life cycle (SDLC). While they were once at the core of development workflows, many CASE tools have since been incorporated into more extensive and specialised software ecosystems. These tools support system design, modelling, code generation and testing, enhancing efficiency and shortening development timelines. Designed to integrate seamlessly into contemporary workflows, CASE tools enable teams to develop high-quality software systems with greater accuracy and reduced error rates.

Typical features provided by CASE tools include:

- support for modelling designs (such as UML diagrams and entity–relationship diagrams);
- code generation (forward engineering) and reverse engineering (generating models from working solutions);
- integration with testing, debugging and deployment tools; and
- workflow automation for SDLC phases.

Typical examples of CASE tools include: IBM Rational Rose, IBM Engineering Workflow Management (formerly Rational Team Concert), Enterprise Architect, Visual Paradigm, ArgoUML, StarUML, MagicDraw and Modelio.

9 DELIVERING DIGITAL SOLUTIONS

This book has sought to decipher the complex discipline of digital solution design by providing a clear framework, practical techniques and real-world examples to help IT professionals, business analysts, project managers and students understand how business requirements are translated into effective, user-focused solutions.

Commencing with an exploration of the objectives, scope and constraints of design work, followed by an analysis of popular design approaches, the book has then taken a deeper dive into the practical aspects of key design elements, including input/output, user interface, process, data, system controls and cybersecurity. It has highlighted the critical role of architecture in digital solution design, covering enterprise, solution and software architecture, discussing architecture policies, principles, standards and patterns that ensure consistency, scalability and alignment with business and technical objectives. The book has concluded with a review of software tools that support digital solution design and architecture.

As the second instalment in a three-part series, this book has bridged the gap between defining requirements (the subject of Book 1) and delivering digital technology (the subject of Book 3), offering a balanced, accessible guide to navigating the challenges of a fast-changing digital world. The final book in the collection (*Delivering Digital Solutions*) continues the journey through the digital solution life cycle by taking a comprehensive look at how digital solutions are built (software engineering), tested and deployed. A sneak preview of *Delivering Digital Solutions* is provided below.

Book 3 in the Digital Solutions Collection is structured into 12 chapters, split across three parts:

- **Chapter 1** picks up where Book 2 left off, revisiting the digital solution life cycle and setting the stage for understanding how the design of a digital solution is realised as working software.

DELIVERING DIGITAL SOLUTIONS

Software engineering, testing and deployment

Peter Thompson

- **Chapter 2** provides an overview of software engineering fundamentals, introducing the software engineering cycle, incorporating coding, testing, debugging and release. It also explores key software engineering principles such as SOLID, DRY and KISS, as well as standards, providing a foundation for disciplined and efficient software development practices.

- **Chapter 3** describes a range of programming paradigms, including procedural, object-oriented, functional and event-driven programming, highlighting their strengths, limitations and typical applications, helping readers to choose the right approach for different aspects of digital solution development.

- **Chapter 4** focuses on the practical implementation of software engineering concepts, discussing modern software development techniques and methods such as modular programming, test-driven development (TDD), DevOps and low-code/no-code development. It also examines critical practices such as version control and managing technical debt, ensuring that software solutions are robust, scalable and maintainable.

- **Chapter 5** explores software development environments, from development and testing to staging and production. It examines how tools such as integrated development environments (IDEs) and continuous integration/delivery (CI/CD) pipelines streamline workflows and promote collaboration during the SDLC.

- **Chapter 6** provides a comprehensive introduction to software testing, covering fundamental concepts, principles and testing types (including functional, performance, security and usability testing). It explains how testing ensures software quality, reduces risk and aligns with design objectives.

- **Chapter 7** builds on testing fundamentals, delving into best practices, such as the shift-left approach, Agile testing and automated testing. It introduces frameworks such as the Agile test pyramid and explains how methodologies like TDD and behaviour-driven development (BDD) integrate testing seamlessly into development workflows.

- **Chapter 8** examines various approaches to deploying digital solutions such as on-premises, cloud, containerised, serverless and edge computing, highlighting their strengths and weaknesses. It also discusses the key factors influencing deployment decisions and explores how these methods align with established frameworks like ITIL, VeriSM and DevOps.

- **Chapter 9** outlines critical considerations and steps involved in successfully deploying digital solutions. Key aspects covered include detailed deployment planning, assessing business and technical readiness, data preparation and user training. It emphasises the importance of clear documentation and careful execution of the deployment process to ensure minimal disruption during the transition to operational use.

- **Chapter 10** discusses various strategies for the changeover to live operational use of the digital solution, such as direct, parallel and phased approaches, along with advanced techniques such as blue/green deployment and canary releases. It highlights the importance of managing risks during the transition to a new digital solution.

- **Chapter 11** explores a range of activities that take place once the solution is operational (maintenance, operations and eventual decommissioning), which completes the coverage of the digital solution life cycle. It addresses the importance of monitoring, updates and user support in maintaining solution effectiveness.

- **Chapter 12** explores a range of software tools used in the development, testing and deployment of digital solutions, from project management and backlog management tools to IDEs, low-code/no-code platforms and CASE tools that streamline software engineering. Computer-aided software testing (CAST) tools automate software testing to enhance quality, while configuration management tools track and manage changes to software. Data management tools facilitate efficient handling of data, supported by ETL tools that integrate and transform data. Finally, DevOps tools, including IaC tools and CI/CD pipelines, enable faster and more reliable deployment through automation.

REFERENCES

Business Architecture Guild. (2024) *A Guide to the Business Architecture Body of Knowledge*® Version 8.5. [BIZBOK® Guide]. Business Architecture Guild.

Chen, P. (1976) 'The entity–relationship model: toward a unified view of data'. In *Proceedings of the 1975 International Conference on Very Large Data Bases*. New York: ACM. 9–36.

Cockburn, A. (2001) *Writing Effective Use Cases*. Boston, MA: Addison-Wesley.

Codd, E.F. (1970) 'A relational model of data for large shared data banks'. *Communications of the ACM*, 13(6). 377–387.

Cooper, A., Reimann, R., Cronin, D., et al. (2014) *About Face: The Essentials of Interaction Design* (4th edition). Chichester: Wiley.

Cross, N. (2006) *Designerly Ways of Knowing*. New York: Springer.

DAMA International. (2017) *DAMA-DMBOK: Data Management Body of Knowledge* (2nd edition). Basking Ridge, NJ: Technics Publications.

Date, C.J. (2004) *An Introduction to Database Systems* (8th edition). Boston, MA: Addison-Wesley.

De Voil, N. (2020) *User Experience Foundations*. Swindon: BCS, The Chartered Institute for IT.

European Commission. (2019) *Ethics guidelines for trustworthy AI*. European Commission High-Level Expert Group on Artificial Intelligence. Available from: digital-strategy. ec.europa.eu/en/library/ethics-guidelines-trustworthy-ai

European Commission. (2021) *Ethics by design and ethics of use approaches for artificial intelligence*. Available from: ec.europa.eu/info/funding-tenders/opportunities/ docs/2021-2027/horizon/guidance/ethics-by-design-and-ethics-of-use-approaches-for-artificial-intelligence_he_en.pdf

Evans, E. (2004) *Domain-Driven Design: Tackling Complexity in the Heart of Software*. Boston, MA: Addison-Wesley.

Gamma, E., Helm, R., Johnson, R., et al. (1994) *Design Patterns: Elements of Reusable Object-Oriented Software*. Boston, MA: Addison-Wesley.

Gordon, K. (2017) *Modelling Business Information: Entity Relationship and Class Modelling for Business Analysts*. Swindon: BCS, The Chartered Institute for IT.

International Organization for Standardization. (1994) *ISO/IEC 7498-1:1994. Information technology – Open Systems Interconnection – Basic reference model: The basic model.* Available from: iso.org/standard/20269.html

International Organization for Standardization. (2004) *ISO/IEC 13335-1:2004. Information technology – Security techniques – Management of information and communications technology security – Part 1: Concepts and models for information and communications technology security management.* Available from: iso.org/standard/39066.html

International Organization for Standardization. (2013) *ISO 27001:2013. Information technology – Security techniques – Information security management systems – Requirements.* Available from: iso.org/standard/54534.html

International Organization for Standardization. (2019) *ISO 9241-210:2019. Ergonomics of human–system interaction – Part 210: Human-centred design for interactive systems.* Available from: iso.org/standard/77520.html

International Organization for Standardization. (2022a) *ISO/IEC 27005:2022. Information security, cybersecurity and privacy protection – Information security risk management.* Available from: iso.org/standard/80585.html

International Organization for Standardization. (2022b) *ISO/IEC 22989:2022. Information technology – Artificial intelligence – Artificial intelligence concepts and terminology.* Available from: iso.org/standard/74296.html

International Organization for Standardization. (2022c) *ISO/IEC 23053:2022. Framework for artificial intelligence (AI) systems using machine learning (ML).* Available from: iso.org/standard/74438.html

International Organization for Standardization. (2022d) *ISO/IEC/IEEE 42010:2022. Software, systems and enterprise – Architecture description.* Available from: iso.org/standard/74393.html

International Organization for Standardization. (2023a) *ISO/IEC 25010:2023. Systems and software engineering – Systems and software quality requirements and evaluation (SQuaRE) – Product quality model.* Available from: iso.org/standard/78176.html

International Organization for Standardization. (2023b) *ISO/IEC 25019:2023. Systems and software engineering – Systems and software quality requirements and evaluation (SQuaRE) – Quality-in-use model.* Available from: iso.org/standard/78177.html

International Software Testing Qualifications Board (ISTQB). (2023) *Certified Tester Foundation Level (CTFL) v4.0.* Syllabus.

Kimball, R. and Ross, M. (2013) *The Data Warehouse Toolkit: The Definitive Guide to Dimensional Modeling* (3rd edition). Chichester: Wiley.

Lovatt, M. (2021) *Solution Architecture Foundations.* Swindon: BCS, The Chartered Institute for IT.

Martin, J. and McClure, C. (1985) *Diagramming Techniques for Analysts and Programmers.* Hoboken, NJ: Prentice-Hall.

National Cyber Security Centre. (2023) *Guidelines for secure AI system development.* Available from: ncsc.gov.uk/collection/guidelines-secure-ai-system-development

National Cyber Security Centre. (2024) *AI and cyber security: what you need to know*. Available from: ncsc.gov.uk/guidance/ai-and-cyber-security-what-you-need-to-know

National Institute of Standards and Technology. (2022) *Secure Software Development Framework (SSDF) Version 1.1: Recommendations for Mitigating the Risk of Software Vulnerabilities*. Washington, DC: US Department of Commerce.

National Institute of Standards and Technology. (2024) *The NIST Cybersecurity Framework (CSF) 2.0*. Washington, DC: US Department of Commerce.

Newman, S. (2020) *Monolith to Microservices: Evolutionary Patterns to Transform Your Monolith*. Sebastopol, CA: O'Reilly.

Nielsen, J. (1994) *10 usability heuristics for user interface design*. Available from: nngroup.com/articles/ten-usability-heuristics

OWASP Foundation. (2021) *OWASP Top 10:2021 – The Ten Most Critical Web Application Security Risks*. Wilmington, DE: OWASP Foundation.

PCI Security Standards Council. (2022) *Payment Card Industry Data Security Standard: Requirements and Testing Procedures, version 4.0*. Wakefield, MA: PCI Security Standards Council.

Sutton, D. (2022) *Cyber Security: The Complete Guide to Cyber Threats and Protection* (2nd edition). Swindon: BCS, The Chartered Institute for IT.

The Open Group. (2022) *The TOGAF® Standard* (10th edition). Hertogenbosch: The Open Group.

Thompson, G., Morgan, P., Samaroo, A., et al. (2024) *Software Testing: An ISTQB-BCS Certified Tester Foundation Level Guide (CTFL v4.0)* (5th edition). Swindon: BCS, The Chartered Institute for IT.

UK Government. (2018) Data Protection Act 2018. Available from: legislation.gov.uk/ukpga/2018/12/contents/enacted

Vernon, V. (2016) *Domain-Driven Design Distilled*. Boston, MA: Addison-Wesley.

World Wide Web Consortium (W3C). (2018) *Web content accessibility guidelines (WCAG) 2.1*. Available from: w3.org/TR/WCAG21

FURTHER READING

Carrie, S. (2024) *Secure Software Design: Safeguarding Your Code Against Cyber Threats*. Self-published.

Girvan, L. and Girvan, S. (2022) *Agile from First Principles*. Swindon: BCS, The Chartered Institute for IT.

IBM. (n.d.) Edgar F. Codd. Available from: ibm.com/history/edgar-codd

IEEE. (1990) *IEEE Standard 610.12-1990. IEEE Standard glossary of software engineering terminology*.

International Institute of Business Analysis (IIBA). (2015) *A Guide to the Business Analysis Body of Knowledge (BABOK® Guide)*. Version 3. Pickering, ON: IIBA.

International Organization for Standardization. (2024) *ISO/IEC/IEEE 41062:2024: Software engineering – Life cycle processes – Software acquisition*.

Martin, R.C. (2000) *Design Principles and Design Patterns*. Gurnee, IL: Object Mentor.

Mellor, S. and Balcer, M.J. (2022) *Executable UML: A Foundation for Model-Driven Architecture*. Boston, MA: Addison-Wesley.

Nielsen, J. (1993) *Usability Engineering*. New York: Academic Press.

North, D. (2006) *Introducing BDD*. Available from: dannorth.net/introducing-bdd/

Paul, D. and Cadle, J. (2020) *Business Analysis* (4th edition). Swindon: BCS, The Chartered Institute for IT.

Richards, M. and Ford, N. (2020) *Fundamentals of Software Architecture: An Engineering Approach*. Sebastopol, CA: O'Reilly.

Ross, J., Beath, C.M. and Mocker, M. (2019) *Designed for Digital: How to Architect Your Business for Sustained Success*. Cambridge, MA: MIT Press.

Rumbaugh, J., Jacobson, I. and Booch, G. (2005) *The Unified Modeling Language Reference Manual* (2nd edition). Boston, MA: Addison-Wesley.

Schwaber, K. and Sutherland, J. (2020) *The Scrum Guide: the definitive guide to Scrum: the rules of the game*. Available from: scrum.org

INDEX

Page numbers in italics refer to figures or tables.

www.ingramcontent.com/pod-product-compliance
Lightning Source LLC
Chambersburg PA
CBHW041007050326
40690CB00031B/5296